An Agenda for the 21st Century

An Agenda for the 21st Century

Rushworth M. Kidder

The MIT Press
Cambridge, Massachusetts
London, England

The interviews in this book were originally published as a series in
The Christian Science Monitor.

© 1987 by The Christian Science Publishing Society

This book was set in Bembo by Achorn Graphic Services and printed and
bound by Halliday Lithograph in the United States of America.

Library of Congress Cataloging-in-Publication Data

An Agenda of the 21st century.

Includes index.
1. Twenty-first century—Forecasts.   I. Kidder, Rushworth M.
CB161.A35 1987   303.4'9'0905   87-22597
ISBN 0-262-11128-4

Contents

Foreword

As the first harbingers of a new century begin to appear, we find ourselves yearning for a peek into the future and to find ways to make it better for our children.

It has become almost a truism to say that, as our present is related to our history, so our future is founded on today. As the 21st century approaches—just thirteen years away— that truism becomes even more true: The next century will be hostage to today's decisions. We have a moral responsibility, therefore, to deal with present issues with as complete as possible an understanding of their impact on the next generations.

In this spirit, *The Christian Science Monitor* presents an agenda for the 21st century. Bringing together a series of interviews with twenty-two leading thinkers published in the daily edition of the *Monitor* between September 1986 and April 1987, this book confronts a single question: What are the major issues mankind will face in the 21st century? Each interviewee was asked that question, and each responded in great detail. Their responses are presented here, along with a summary article distilling the six issues they most frequently mentioned: the need to counter the nuclear threat, the population crisis, and the degradation of the environment; to bridge the gap between the industrial nations and the third world; and to stem the decline in education and reverse the breakdown of public and private morality.

Why does a newspaper get involved in such a project? In the largest sense, this book is an effort to be responsive to the mission established for the *Monitor* by its founder, Mary Baker Eddy, who wrote in its first issue (25 November 1908), "The object of the *Monitor* is to injure no man but to bless all mankind."

That is a challenging mandate. Over the years it has led this newspaper not only to report the news of the day but to promote understanding—between races, between nations, between haves and have-nots, between generations, and now between centuries. It has encouraged us to present current events with courage, clarity, and compassion, striving to be as objective as possible and to consider the background surrounding an event, the developing trends, and the implications for the future. And it has caused us to focus on highlighting possible solutions to world problems.

So when the concept for a series of interviews on the future with leading thinkers began to take shape in the spring of 1986, it seemed a natural extension of our established practice. Aware that the expectations for the future needed to be realistic, we also recognized that the appraisal of the future must not be so encumbered by present limitations that it lack vision. Our job, we soon recognized, was to seek out individuals who could articulate a sense of vision within a realistic framework. We were not looking only for optimists, however, but for those whose visions of the future could help "bless all mankind" even when they included grave and disturbing warnings.

Months before the interviewing began, we spent uncounted hours in discussion of the project. First, we recognized that for overall consistency and balance we needed a single interviewer who was a generalist rather than a specialist in any one field. We selected Rushworth Kidder, a *Monitor* reporter, editor, and writer of the weekly "Perspectives" column, who has done a number of special series and reports. His background in literature (he holds a Ph.D. in English from Columbia University and spent ten years as an English professor at Wichita State University in Kansas before joining the *Monitor* as London correspondent in 1979), as well as his undergraduate training in biochemistry and his long-standing interest in music and art, qualified him well for the wide range of backgrounds he encountered in the individuals he interviewed.

Next we thought through the overall tone and approach of the series. One approach to writing about the 21st century might have been to dazzle the reader with the technological developments that will transform the lives of the citizens of the new era. Certainly those things have an important role in these pages. But our focus has been less on technological wizardry itself than on the social impact of the new inventions. Although we did not slant the interviews that way, we found that again and again our interviewees felt strongly that life in the 21st century would not be shaped simply by technology but by humanity's ability to come to terms with the social impact of new inventions.

The next step was to develop a list of candidates for these interviews. As we narrowed the list down from several hundred promising suggestions, we sought a balance of nationality, political viewpoints, gender, religions, and race. We chose some well-known and some lesser-known individuals. Some readers may wonder why a favorite sage has not been included. We make no claim to have compiled a comprehensive list of superior thinkers. Instead, we sought diversity, a range of views and specialties, as we interviewed philosophers, politicans, economists, social scientists, artists, educators, physicists, business people, and authors.

Finally, we committed a significant amount of space to the project, in order to given each individual room to express his or her views in depth. The result was one of the most extensive single series in the paper's history—and, to judge by the volume and tone of the mail, one of the most enthusiastically received by our readers.

Prominent among the readers' responses was a sense of appreciation to the thinkers themselves for their depth of insight—and to the newspaper for distilling such complex issues into an understandable framework and for helping to set priorities. My own years as a board member and current president of the American Society of Newspaper Editors convince me that readers will expect newspapers to play a major role in addressing the complexities of the coming century. As advancing technology multiplies the sources of information, the public will continually be bombarded by masses of disconnected information—available not only in print and electronic modes but in new forms that merge the familiar media types. The responsible press must make some sense out of all this to help readers find paths through the often confusing maze of facts and opinion.

But ultimately it is the readers who will have to put to use the material provided by the press. This book does not attempt to provide solutions for all the problems it raises. Where individual interviewees had suggestions for a better future, we were eager to include them. Our goal, however, was simply to set forth the agenda from the perspective of 1987 so that we could devote special attention to the issues of greatest concern. We may want to revise and amend our agenda as other issues surge to the forefront during the closing years of this century.

Agendas never accomplish anything until they are acted upon. The next step is to press on toward solutions. We believe that each individual has an urgent responsibility to consider the impact of today's decisions and the ends to which our actions are tending. It was with this intent that we began our search for a vision of the future that can help enlighten it. That enlightenment will take effect in proportion as each reader, building upon the wisdom of this collection of thinkers, begins to form his or her own agenda for the 21st century.

Katherine Fanning
Editor
The Christian Science Monitor

Acknowledgments

Some books are efforts of single-minded inspiration. Others reflect the work of many hands. This one is very much in the latter camp, and the debts to those who made it possible are manifold.

To my colleagues at *The Christian Science Monitor* I owe more than I can possibly articulate. The germ of the idea first surfaced in an internal memo written by Richard Ralston to John Hoagland, manager of The Christian Science Publishing Society. Katherine Fanning and David Anable (the editor and the managing editor, respectively, of the *Monitor*) had the insight to see the promise in that memo. They set me to work refining it for a series of articles, and the three of us devoted countless hours of invaluable discussion to the project.

As the work got under way, the entire writing staff of the paper was solicited for the names of potential interviewees. Responsibility for editing the series fell to the wise and gentle hands of Roderick Nordell; Peter Spotts and Gregory Lamb shepherded it into print with many helpful observations; and Kirsten Conover undertook the considerable amount of secretarial work with unfailing skill and cheerfulness. The series moved into book form under the steady guidance of John Hoagland and Tom Fuller.

To the twenty-two interviewees themselves, of course, go my particular thanks. They invariably seized the significance of the task. They challenged themselves to bring lifetimes of deep thought to bear on an unwieldy and undefined topic—the long-range future of humanity—and they did so with grace, enthusiasm, and precision. More than that, they spoke with a conviction that their ideas would make a difference. Several of them suggested some fine tuning of their own words after these interviews had been done. These changes, along with an editorial decision to smooth out the prose by removing some of the brackets inside quotation marks where the meaning was clear, account for the slight difference between the interviews as originally published and as they appear here.

Finally, a special note of thanks to my wife and family. They, too, saw and supported the purpose behind the project. They helped me see it in broad perspective. But most of all, through the years, they taught me to listen, to care, and to share—qualities upon which good interviews, like good families, are founded.

Camden, Maine
June 1987

Introduction:
Toward a New Agenda

What's on the world's agenda for the 21st century? What are the fundamental issues that humanity must address if the 21st century is to be a viable age? Which ones are of first intensity, and which important but secondary?

As the twentieth century spins toward the year 2000, those questions are increasingly being posed. Never mind that the turn of the century, and of the millennium, is still more than a decade away: The market is already flooded with books, magazine stories, journal articles, radio talk shows, and television documentaries with the beguiling and faintly disquieting number *2000* in their titles. Some of them offer barely credible profiles of a superprosperous "sci-fi" age. Others are filled with doomsday forebodings. Many see both gathering clouds and rays of hope.

Why this upsurge of interest in the future?

One answer is that the ends of centuries, like the ends of each passing year, call forth a kind of societal soul-searching—moments for reflection, times for taking stock of what's behind and pondering what's ahead, occasions for making new resolutions. That, at least, was the tenor of the decade preceding the end of the 19th century. And in those days there seemed to be much to be concerned about: an upsurge in bohemianism, the spread of yellow journalism, the seeping away of religious values, the ferment over women's rights, the rising tides of nationalism, the challenge to colonialism, industrial monopoly, and scores of other issues.

Yet to us that period may look like a model of stability. What our grandparents could only vaguely imagine—world wars, weapons of mass destruction, appalling genocide—soon came to pass. Some of the most prominent achievements of the 20th century—the creation of entire nations of economically privileged *majorities* rather than *minorities,* the crumbling of racial segregation, the new sensitivity to environmental pollution—were not even on the 19th century's agenda. Nor were the technologies of television and air travel—which, by shrinking the world into what Marshall McLuhan aptly called a "global village," have perhaps done more than anything else to bring humankind together elbow to elbow.

But listen to what one of the 19th century's most celebrated American astronomers thought about air travel. "No possible combination of known substances, known forms of machinery and known forms of force," asserted Simon Newcomb early in this century, "can be united in a practical machine by which men shall fly long distances through the air."

Novelist and futurist Arthur C. Clarke, quoting Newcomb in his book *Profiles of the Future,* draws the moral from this story. "With monotonous regularity," Clarke writes, "apparently competent men have laid down the law about what is technically possible or impossible—and have been proved utterly wrong, sometimes while the ink was scarcely dry from their pens."[1] He goes so far as to deduce what he calls Clarke's First Law, which is: "When a distinguished but elderly scientist states that something is possible he is almost certainly right. When he states that something is impossible, he is very probably wrong."[2]

Then what's so special about today's concern for 2000 and beyond? Is it any different from the speculations of our ancestors? Does our fascination arise simply from the rolling over of three zeroes following the number 2—as though we had hit the jackpot on some cosmic slot machine? Or is there a special reason for our concern? In other words, is *our* age different?

Yes and no, say the current generation of forward thinkers. We are, of course, still capable of going wildly awry in our predictions. Yet never before have the forces of change been so concentrated, the pace so blistering, the issues so world embracing. Never before, according to a number of today's historians, pundits, and prophets, has humanity appeared to hold such power—for vast improvement or for utter devastation—over its own future.

Alvin Toffler describes the experience of this power with his now-famous label "future shock"—which he calls an "abrupt collision with the future" by people unprepared for it.[3] Putting that shock into historical perspective, he notes that the last fifty thousand years of man's existence can be divided up into about eight hundred "lifetimes" of sixty-two years each. "Only during the last seventy lifetimes," he writes, "has it been possible to communicate effectively from one lifetime to another—as writing made it possible to do. Only during the last six lifetimes did masses of men ever see a printed word. Only during the last four has it been possible to measure time with any precision. Only in the last two has anyone anywhere used an electric motor. And the overwhelming majority of all the material goods we use in daily life today have been developed within the present, the eight-hundredth, lifetime."[4]

Marvin Cetron and Thomas O'Toole, expanding on this idea of fast-paced change in *Encounters with the Future,* cite the Confucian adage that "only the supremely wise and abysmally ignorant do not change."[5]

"No matter how old you are in the year 2000," they write, "profound change will have been written into your life by the time you start the 21st century. None of us will be the same when the century turns. If the dramatic change of the sixties is not in the air these days, do not for one minute think that change is not on its way."[6]

Some find the change exhilarating. Social forecaster John Naisbitt, author of *Megatrends,* describes our age as *"the time of the parenthesis, the time between eras."*

"It is as though we have bracketed off the present from both the past and the future," he writes, "for we are neither here nor there. . . . Although the time between eras is uncertain, it is a great and yeasty time, filled with opportunity. If we can learn to make uncertainty our friend, we can achieve much more than in stable eras."[7]

Others, however, take a far more sobering view. Richard D. Lamm, former governor of Colorado, worries that "Our basic, long-term problems are not being solved— they are being covered over. The future, in fact, is much bigger, darker, and more problematical than anything our bright new technology can dominate."[8] Across the Atlantic, a team of British authors forecasting America's future for the next decade notes that "the indications are disturbing . . . that the *dominant vision* of the next decade will most likely be one of strident individualism lacking in the idealism or moral conviction necessary to do more than muddle through."[9]

And George Gallup Jr., drawing together survey results in *Forecast 2000,* writes, "just beneath the surface of our society, a great historical tidal wave is on the move—a set of monumental political, social, and economic impulses, which are carrying us relentlessly toward a rendezvous with the future."[10]

"I'm sufficiently convinced that our society is heading in a dangerous direction," Gallup concludes, "that I feel compelled to sound a note of extreme urgency."[11]

Again and again, in both the published writings of the age's forward-looking thinkers and the interviews collected in this book, that sense of urgency emerges. But the goal is a luminous one: to alert humanity, to awaken thought, to focus attention on the central issues.

And what *are* those issues? There are hundreds out there to choose from. Should we pour our attention into fighting drugs or controlling deficit spending, battling alcoholism or the ozone layer, remedying the glut of lawyers or the dearth of engineers? Should we worry about farm foreclosures or the greenhouse effect, solid waste or budgetary waste, women's rights or leveraged buyouts, the bottom-line mentality or the top-secret mentality? Will the future be defined by terrorism, teenage pregnancy, or trade protectionism? One thing seems sure: For each of these, and for scores of others, individuals and special-interest groups can be found who will argue that their particular topic is the most important issue since the invention of the crossbow.

What are we to make of this swirl of competing issues? British literary critic Raymond Williams, posing a striking image for our age, likens it to "a cluttered room in which somebody is trying to think, while there is a fan-dance going on in one corner and a military band blasting away in the other." The result, he writes, is "a systematic cacophony which may indeed not be bright enough to know that it is jamming and drowning the important signals."[12]

This book, quite simply, is an effort to listen to those "important signals." Its ultimate goal is to articulate the agenda of first-intensity issues that emerges from the twenty-two interviews that follow. These thinkers do not necessarily offer answers—although, where promising solutions and potential ways forward emerge, they point them out. Instead, their purpose is to focus the attention and energies of mankind on the handful of vital concerns that must top the agenda for the 21st century.

Notes

1. *Profiles of the Future* (New York: Holt, Rinehart and Winston, 1984), p. 16.

2. *Ibid.*, p. 29.

3. *Future Shock* (New York: Bantam Books, 1971), p. 9.

4. *Ibid.*, p. 14.

5. *Encounters with the Future: A Forecast of Life into the 21st Century* (New York: McGraw-Hill, 1983), p. 19.

6. *Ibid.*, p. 21.

7. *Megatrends: Ten New Directions Transforming Our Lives* (New York: Warner Books, 1982), pp. 249, 252.

8. *Megatraumas: America at the Year 2000* (Boston: Houghton Mifflin, 1985), p. 2.

9. David R. Young et al., *America in Perspective* (Boston: Houghton Mifflin, 1986), p. 369.

10. George Gallup Jr. and William Proctor, *Forecast 2000* (New York: William Morrow, 1984), p. 11.

11. *Ibid.*, p. 156.

12. *The Year 2000* (New York: Pantheon Books, 1983), p. 18.

Attempting the Impossible

I

Be realistic: Attempt the impossible
—graffito at the Sorbonne, noted by Mortimer Adler

Mortimer Adler

Sissela Bok

Shuichi Kato

Michael K. Hooker

Mortimer Adler

Philosopher of Practical Wisdom

It may well be true, as Hamlet told Horatio, that "there are more things in heaven and earth . . . than are dreamt of in your philosophy." Philosophy, nevertheless, at least begins to dream about those things—which is why it seems fitting to launch an examination of the 21st century with the views of philosophers.

The four individuals in this section—Mortimer Adler, Sissela Bok, Shuichi Kato, and Michael Hooker—come out of varied backgrounds. But they have in common a fascination with the great shaping ideas of the past that, in their view, will continue to guide humanity into the future. Adler puts the point succinctly: "I've learned slowly," he says, "that practical wisdom consists in taking the longest view of things you can."

For Adler—university professor, author of some thirty books, chairman of the board of editors of the Encyclopaedia Brittanica, co-compiler (with Robert Maynard Hutchins) of the fifty-four-volume Great Books of the Western World, and gem in the crown of the Aspen Institute for Humanistic Studies—that kind of wisdom has not always come in ordinary ways.

He earned his Ph.D. from Columbia University in 1928— but his B.A. only in 1983, when Columbia finally waived a swimming requirement that Adler had refused to pass as a student. He never graduated from high school, quitting DeWitt Clinton High

School in the Bronx (he was born in New York City) before getting a diploma. Married in 1963, he has two children.

True to his Aristotelian training, Adler's concern focuses on ideas. A recent book, Six Great Ideas (1981), devotes it chapters to truth, goodness, beauty, liberty, equality, and justice. Earlier, in the famous two-volume Syntopicon, he indexed 102 great ideas found in 443 works by 74 authors. His "popularizing" tendencies long ago caused him to part ways with academic philosophers. But he remains convinced that philosophy can be more than a merely scholarly pursuit, and he now pushes strenuously for educational reform, demonstrating through the seminars he occasionally teaches that even young students can be trained to think deeply.

Now director of the Institute for Philosophical Research in Chicago, the former University of Chicago professor still rises very early each day to get to his writing. His most recent book, We Hold These Truths: Understanding the Ideas and Ideals of the Constitution, is a philosopher's study of the Constitution of the United States.

Aspen, Colorado

During the student revolts in Paris in the late 1960s, a lot of graffiti appeared on the walls of the Sorbonne.

"One youngster," recalls Mortimer Adler, who tells the story with a chuckle, "put on the wall, 'Be realistic: Attempt the impossible.' "

"That's a wonderful statement," he concludes.

With more than half a century as a philosopher behind him, Professor Adler still delights in such forward-looking iconoclasm. He explained why in an interview at his summer residence—seated in shirt sleeves at his kitchen table, oblivious of the cat that now and then steps on the tape recorder and rubs up against his arm.

As Adler looks toward the 21st century, he sees two

---

central issues topping the agenda for America—neither of which lends itself to solution within traditional frameworks.

The first is an urgent need to challenge, dismantle, and rebuild one of the most solidly entrenched institutions in the nation: the educational establishment.

"Our educational system is absolutely inadequate—not relatively but absolutely inadequate—for the purposes of democracy," he says forcefully. "That's the No. 1 agenda item. If we don't solve the educational problem—if we have only the kinds of citizens we have now—forget it."

The second issue is what he calls "the problem of the national debt, which mortgages our future." The United States, he says, has been described as "the largest debtor nation in the world, by far," and there's "no indication that we have any control of the thing at the moment."

"These, I think, are, for this country, the great questions for the next century."

The first of the issues, educational reform, is the subject through which Adler is perhaps most widely known. His long association with the Great Books program has brought his name into discussion groups all over the country. As the driving force behind a group of twenty-three reform-minded American educators, he helped design the Paideia Proposal, wrote the trilogy of books setting forth this plan for a different sort of primary and secondary education, and has pushed for its adoption in public school systems around the country.

The Paideia Proposal—which he pronounces *pie-DAY-ya,* borrowing the term from a Greek word for the upbringing of children—calls for a curriculum with few electives. It divides classroom activity at all levels into three distinct dimensions: the acquisition of information, the coaching of students by teachers, and the give-and-take of Socratic questioning. It emphasizes training in critical thinking through vigorous student discussion and interchange.

That may sound like a return to the Three Rs of old-school basics, and in some ways it is. But Adler's goal is not education for education's sake. He sees in improved education nothing short of the salvation of democracy—a subject about which he speaks with something of the first-generation American's fervor.

"I'm a firm believer that democracy is the only perfectly just form of government in terms of what human beings are." But to make it work, he adds, "we have to make the citizens recognize their moral and intellectual responsibilities. I've often said that if this is impossible, then we ought to give democracy up."

And why is an educated citizenry so important?

"If you take democracy seriously," he answers, you find that "the citizens are the ruling class. The guys in Washington are their servants. We, the people, are the government."

It is on this point—citizens as rulers—that Adler builds his case for education.

"What most Americans don't realize is that political democracy . . . is not yet fifty years old in this country. The notion that this country was founded as a democracy, of course, is sheer rot. It was anything but that: It was an oligarchy of the most severe kind."

In fact, says Adler, democracy in America is "so recent, both in terms of constitutional amendments and in terms of legislative enactments, that the problem for the next century for us is to make it work."

For Adler this means education, of both mind and moral character.

Moral character is also an aspect of the second major item on Adler's 21st-century agenda—the problem of national debt.

He links the problem, in part, to the superpower relationship. And he contends that the problem will not be resolved "unless we do something about removing the threat of nuclear war and reducing the expenditure for armed forces" through some sort of mutual agreement between the United States and the Soviet Union.

In the end, however, the debt problem transcends the question of superpower relations. Like so much else in Adler's view, it traces itself at last to a moral problem—arising, in this case, from the very affluence of the nation.

"It is more difficult to become morally virtuous under affluent conditions than under adverse conditions," says Adler, expounding an idea whose roots lie deep in the classical philosophy in which he is so thoroughly steeped.

"Adversity is a better prod of development of moral character than affluence. Take any family. Children of affluent families are often ruined by the affluence that surrounds them. Everything is too easy."

"I'm not recommending hardship," he says. "I'm only saying it's more difficult" to raise what he calls "morally virtuous young people" under such conditions.

"If you said to many people today, 'You really have to suffer stringent reductions of your standard of living for the sake of your grandchildren and your grandchildren's grandchildren, since we can't go on spending the way we're spending,' they would be morally incapable of doing that."

Yet that kind of austerity, he feels, is just what's needed to control debt on a national scale.

The debt problem, for Adler, is related more to the success of American democracy than to any sense of economic failure. And he has no reservations about the significance of that success.

"Let me put it to you this way," he says, with a born teacher's eagerness to explain. "Up until 1900, in every country in the world, you had privileged minorities and oppressed majorities, correct? In the 20th century, in the United States, for the first time you had a privileged majority. Let's suppose we now have 15 million really destitute persons—illiterate, ill-kempt, ill-nourished. That's a very small portion of the country—terrible, but it's a small portion of the population, considering the vast number of 240 million who are, on the whole, well off. We have given those 240 million, the vast majority, all the conditions of a good life."

In many ways, in fact, "this is the best of centuries. You and I can't even imagine what it's going to be like at the end of the century in terms of technological progress. All that is on the side of a brighter future."

If, that is, we can manage the debt problem.

What about Adler's agenda for the rest of the world?

"The agenda for the world, I would think, puts world peace at the top, the prevention of nuclear devastation."

Adler emphasizes, however, that "the world must understand peace as something other than a negative condition, which is the absence of fighting. Peace, as a positive condition, is that situation in which individuals and peoples can solve all their problems, all their conflicts, by law and by talk rather than by force.

"That has been said by the wisest men of all times. But how do you do that? You do it only through the operation of the machinery of government. Wherever you have peace positively, you have civil peace. And civil peace is the product of civil government—the use of law and authorized force to maintain peace."

And that, he says, is something different from the armed truce between sovereign states that is sometimes known as peace.

In addition to the need for peace, Adler's international agenda carries four other global issues: environmental pollution, population pressures, energy supply, and what he calls "the fundamental conflict" between "the have and have-not nations."

"Those are four big problems to solve," he says, noting that each one is global in scope. "They won't be solved by [individual] national governments, none of them," he asserts.

Are they, then, insoluble? Not at all, Adler says. "I don't think any of these problems is intellectually as difficult as putting a man on the moon," he says, adding, "we solved that fairly well."

He notes, however, that the "cold, clear, rational thinking" that produced the moon walk was unhampered by a host of other human failings, which he lumps under the general heading of "folly and vice." His list includes unenlightened self-interest, blind passions, hatred of foreigners, irrational racial and ethnic prejudices, and short-term profit seeking. "If we can do the same kind of cold, clear, rational thinking about our moral, social, political, and economic problems, we could solve them."

Isn't that a tall order for humanity? Adler concedes as much. He notes, however, that while he is "a short-term pessimist" he remains a "long-term optimist."

"I don't think we're going to solve any of these problems in this century, and maybe not in the next. And things are going to get worse before they get better. And one of the reasons why they'll get better is because when they get bad enough we'll do something about it."

If, in his eight decades of experience, one way forward seems particularly promising, it is the concept of a world federal government—an organization that would be broad enough to handle problems that have become increasingly global.

"Back in the '40s and '50s," Adler says, "I argued for world government simply in terms of preventing war. I think the argument now is much stronger."

Why? Because through television and air travel, "the whole earth is smaller—not geographically, but in terms of communication and travel—than the thirteen colonies were in 1787 when they formed 'a more perfect union,' " he says, quoting from the preamble to the Constitution.

"Think of the amount of time it took [in 1787] for a letter to get from Boston to Charleston, South Carolina. Think of how long it took the delegates to get to the Continental Congress or the convention in Philadelphia." Now, he points out, a group of leaders from around the world "could all meet in Geneva tomorrow."

But, if they were to meet, could they overcome the human penchant for "folly and vice" and arrive at some solutions? Or would that be impossible?

"When we say that something is impossible, we're in exactly the same situation of our ancestors looking at us and saying, 'We can't believe it, that's impossible.'

"The word *impossible* is a very strong word. When you say, *Impossible!* you ought to say, 'relative to my present state of ignorance, it's impossible.' "

Sissela Bok

Grappling with Principles

"I feel very strongly," says social philosopher Sissela Bok, about "exemplary human lives. That doesn't mean perfect human lives but just human beings who tried harder than many others to live up to their principles."

Humanity's ability to grapple with "principles" has engaged Bok's attention for years. Her doctoral dissertation at Harvard was a study of voluntary euthanasia, and her two best-known books— Lying: Moral Choice in Public and Private Life *(1978) and* Secrets: On the Ethics of Concealment and Revelation *(1983)—explore challenges arising when individuals and societies confront vexing problems of morality.*

Her interest in such questions reflects her upbringing in a family where both parents were deeply involved in social causes. Her father, Gunnar Myrdal, won the Nobel Memorial Prize in Economics in 1974. Eight years later her mother, Swedish diplomat Alva Myrdal, won the Nobel Peace Prize for her work on disarmament. Bok studied in Sweden, Switzerland, and at the Sorbonne, where she met her husband, Derek C. Bok, now president of Harvard University.

Bok, who has taught classes in ethics at the Harvard Medical School and the John F. Kennedy School of Government, teaches courses in humanities and ethics at Brandeis University. Her latest book, A Strategy for Peace, *is based on a series of lectures on human values and the threat of war given at the Erikson Center of the Cambridge Hospital.*

Cambridge, Massachusetts

On first glance, Sissela Bok's agenda for the 21st century appears to be crowded with items. In a gently spoken English flavored with the accents of her native Sweden, she touches on a whole litany of problems that humanity will face in the next century: nuclear weaponry, world poverty, disease, illiteracy, unemployment, poor housing, the breakup of the family, child abuse, the atmosphere's ozone layer, and more.

But above these, she says, "there are really two overarching challenges."

"The first one—which is absolutely crucial, because if we don't meet that we're not going to *have* a 21st century—is the problem of violence."

The second centers on the fact that "our technological advances have been so extraordinary that they have to some extent left us behind when it comes to the wisdom of using all that we are now capable of using."

Bok is deeply interested is solutions, in what she calls the "underlying needs" of the next century. Standing out clearly in her thinking are the twin needs of developing "trust" among individuals and nations and then of creating "the actual institutions for resolving problems and negotiating difficulties."

Reduced to its essence, her agenda has one item on it: the issue of trust. Why? "Because trust is, if anything, absolutely as important as the ozone layer for our survival."

Trust, to this student of ethics, has nothing Pollyannaish about it. She looks askance at the word when it is mouthed by statesmen who do not demonstrate it through their actions. To Bok, trust is something built up among

---

individuals and nations by repeated actions—a basis for relations that are deep enough to permit negotiated settlements of the world's outstanding difficulties.

"There are a great many problems in our society that we absolutely have to work *together* at," she says, "and it is not possible to work together at them so long as there is so very much distrust."

In a morning's conversation in the elegant library of her pre-Revolutionary house in Cambridge, where poet James Russell Lowell once lived, she builds her case carefully and thoughtfully.

"In the 20th century," she says, "we have had more brutal forms of persecution and of violence than possibly any other century has known." In particular, "there have been people who have written about violence—the greatness of violence, and of persecution, and of bias—like Hitler and Mussolini. And of course," she adds, referring to the 20th-century use of concentration camps and the development of nuclear weapons, "we've had methods that no other century has known, either."

But she notes that such violence "has found a countervailing response that I think is possibly even more extraordinary, which is the practice of nonviolent resistance."

She acknowledges "a long tradition, certainly in religion and in philosophy, of nonviolence." But she says that "the new aspect . . . in the 20th century has been the conscious use of nonviolent resistance to counter oppression and injustice and persecution."

She cites Mohandas Gandhi and Martin Luther King, and, currently, Corazon Aquino, whom she praises for trying to carry on the nonviolent tradition.

But Gandhi and King, she says, were concerned not only with changing the large issues that affected entire societies. They were also "very, very much concerned . . . with personal change among a great many individuals. And they were concerned with trying to counteract violence in one's personal life, in one's community.

"Gandhi used the expression, I think, of 'zones of peace.' If one could make one's self into a more peaceful individual, if one could try to extend that into one's family, one would already have done quite a lot. If one could do something within the community, and perhaps within one's society, and keep very much open to the possibility of trying, however hard it is, to do it for the entire world—it's this idea of forming a small zone and pushing outward that I think is very impressive."

Does this lead her to feel that pacifist movements will have a strong role to play in the 21st century?

"I think that almost all approaches that try to move toward peace have something to be said for them," she says. "But one problem I guess I see . . . with many peace movements all over the world, is that they are so focused on weapons.

"I certainly would say that we have to do something about weapons—we have to move toward disarmament, absolutely. But that is far from the only approach that we have to take. I think, if anything, it's more important to work at the political attitudes that nations have toward one another, and the various political actions that they choose to take.

"The only way it's going to be possible to face up to that [problem of violence], I believe, is somehow to manage to reduce the distrust that presently exists and that makes it impossible to seek collective solutions."

Bok stresses a warning from the introduction of a book she is working on: "Merely to call for greater trust and kindliness, as many do, however, is once again useless, so long as the present strong reasons for distrust remain. Clearly, governments are right in not taking anything at face value when the stakes are so high. Caution and distrust will always serve national self-protection, and lapsing into naïve trust . . . would be the height of folly."

But the reasons for distrust can be reduced. "There are many things that governments do that diminish trust all the time," she says. "And it's in those areas that I think we have to try to put pressure on governments to stop doing those things."

Trust-diminishing actions include "such things as being unreliable with respect to treaties, being unreliable with respect to information—issuing disinformation, for instance—and undertaking various forms of hostility, subversively or secretly, that can only increase the distrust between nations.

"I think it's very difficult just to have [superpower] negotiations with respect to arms, while you're constantly undercutting the country in all these other ways."

Of particular concern to Bok is the fact that such actions, which in themselves may seem innocuous, produce a cumulative erosion and slowly create distrust.

"There are many people," she says, who have simply "given up. They're not in the peace movement—they're not in any kind of movement. They've given up on the question of world peace, and they have often given up on their government. They may not be voting." Such people probably constitute "the greatest danger" to the governments of the future. Why? Because "being so passive, they will in the long run be much more easily manipulated.

"It can happen that someone can come along who is . . . quite a charismatic person and a demagogue," she explains. Such a person "can manipulate those people who had allowed themselves to be so uninformed, because they care so little and because they are so much in despair about world events. They don't even read the newspaper very often. They are so uninformed that if someone comes and tells them something that really is a barefaced piece of misinformation, they may believe it—and they may get drawn into all kinds of forms of violence, or of hatred of nationalities or races.

"The right attitude is to try to build a zone of peace or trust—and then not to assume that everything outside is lies and broken promises and manipulation." That assumption, she says, "really is a calumny on the many public leaders" who are genuinely trying to create trust.

"In the 21st century," she says, "if, as I do believe, the issue of trust is so central, then government leaders are going to have to systematically think through what kinds of actions increase trust, and what kinds of actions decrease it.

"What that's going to mean, is that officials will have to take moral principles into account—whether or not they really want to." They will have to realize that "the principles are important from their own point of view of survival— whatever their own personal moral views are. They're going to have to realize that if they want to be trusted, if they want to be able to negotiate, if they want to try to solve some of these important problems that maybe they're going to manage to solve, they're going to have to do it on a basis of trust."

And that, says Bok, leads to the "other big change that we're going to have to undertake"—the need to support international institutions.

"It's not going to be possible in the 21st century for countries to go it alone, so to speak, and expect that these vast, overarching problems will be solved," she says. "I feel that we have to be . . . much more supportive of international organizations and of what some people call interdependence—the notion, the acknowledgment, that we are dependent on really everyone else in the world."

Needed, she says, is a strengthening of "an international framework that now is very hampered." She worries that "there's been a tremendous pulling back" from international organizations by the United States.

"We need to support the World Court," she says, and "to accept its decisions"—a reference to the Reagan administration's refusal to accept the court's jurisdiction in a case involving Nicaraguan charges against the United States in 1985. "So should the Soviet Union, once again in its own long-run best interest."

She also notes that "we need to play an important role in the United Nations," despite the fact that "the United Nations is not all that one might hope."

"All those international organizations, in all their many ways discussing all the different issues—they are what we have," she says simply.

This interdependence—and the realization that what seem to be separate items on the agenda are all interconnected—is "something that we've discovered more and more during the 20th century."

That interconnectedness, for Bok, has two sides. On the positive side, she notes that her father, Gunnar Myrdal, a prime architect of the Swedish welfare state, called such interconnectedness "a virtuous circle."

"We know about vicious circles, where everything just goes down and down and down. But there is also the possibility of sparking an action with respect to something, for instance, like civil rights." Such an action may reach far beyond its small beginnings and touch scores of interrelated problems—housing, education, disease control, and so forth.

The dark side of this interconnectedness is what Bok calls "the danger of defeatism and passivity." If "everything is connected with everything else," some people may ask, " 'What's the use of doing anything, where do I come in?'

"Here is where I think again it's so important to say that what any individual does will make some small difference. If it is working for the homeless or working with the aged, working within your own family with a sick child, working to improve your relationship with a brother or a sister, or in the community or in the nation—those activities, small as they may be, can have an effect, if only a marginal effect, on the largest questions."

Shuichi Kato

Encouraging Compassion

Shuichi Kato appears to be having a lover's quarrel with Japan.

On the one hand, he is the author of a prize-winning history of Japanese literature and enough other writing (most of it about Japan) to fill fifteen volumes of collected works.

On the other hand, he cherishes his "marginal" position in Japanese society, where, as moralist and social critic, he speaks out frequently against consumerism, groupism, educational inflexibility, male chauvinism, and other deep-rooted elements in Japanese culture.

How did a society he describes as "subtle, rigid, and controlled" produce such a maverick?

The son of a doctor, he recalls that "I was very often sick as a child, so that I stayed home. I didn't go to the school for many months. And this was a kind of a sanctuary."

Then in 1951 he "escaped" to France and, later, to Canada. "Altogether after the war," he says, "I have spent my life half outside of Japan."

Trained as a doctor, Kato held a position as hematologist with the Tokyo University Clinic until 1959. Having written poetry and fiction since the end of World War II, however, he found medicine too specialized.

So around 1960, as he once told an interviewer, he gave up

medicine and "decided to become a specialist in nonspecialization."
Since then he has spent much of his time teaching—at Yale, Brown,
and Cambridge universities, as well as at universities in West Ger-
many, Switzerland, and Mexico. From 1976 to 1985 he was a
professor of comparative culture at Sophia University in Tokyo.

Tokyo

In one sense, Shuichi Kato is characteristically Japanese. As
his visitors remove their shoes in the entryway of his modest
home in the once-rural outskirts of Tokyo, he offers them
slippers. With ritual bows, he exchanges business cards. Part-
way through the interview that follows, his wife slips into the
room with tea and cookies.

But the entryway shelves are filled with English-
language books. His business cards are hand-painted in
China. The interview, in English, is enriched by quotations
from Bertrand Russell and Graham Greene. And the tea is a
sweet, strong, fruity decoction, quite unlike the pale green
brew usually served on such occasions.

For Kato (pronounced *KAH-toh*) is hardly typical of his
countrymen. Sometimes described as "the moral conscience
of Japan," he is outspoken but calm, keenly logical but
deeply intuitive. He makes it clear that the carefully calibrated
traditions and attitudes of Japan—and of much of the rest
of the world—will need to undergo serious changes in the
21st century.

"Most people are not very much concerned, seriously,
with other people's suffering," he says. "By and large it
seems to me that the whole of society is geared to domination
and manipulation rather than to compassion."

He is concerned that the news and advertising media are
constantly portraying a "striving for power, money, and
domination of other people." Rarely does the public hear

about a government or a corporation "doing something motivated by a compassion for other people's suffering."

How, he is asked, can the world bring more of the moral conscience to bear on the issues before it?

"It's very difficult," he responds. "Perhaps, to fight back, we should make efforts to take control, to resist that desire [to manipulate]—and also to help, to encourage, to reinforce all actions motivated by compassion for others.

"The 21st century will be inhabited by people whom we don't know, whose mentalities and abilities are very different," he continues. However much we may wish for "blueprints" of the future, "we cannot get rid of our limitations and our scope as 20th-century man." Yet, although we "don't know the way in which future people will *handle* the problems, perhaps we can anticipate to some extent the problems themselves."

"I think the history of nuclear arms from 1945 until now makes inevitable the progress in quality and increases in quantity. I don't see any reason in the future why this technological progress will stop."

For several reasons, then, he expects that the future will be "more dangerous" and "less secure." First, there will be "a greater probability of errors and mistakes" as technology grows more complicated. Second, there will be an "obvious gap" between machines and the people controlling them. Although technology has been developing rapidly, he sees little progress in "the whole social organization and ability of the human race to control its own products."

Equally troublesome, he notes, will be nuclear waste disposal. He worries, in particular, about the "accumulated effect" of nuclear waste, unless nations find immediate solutions.

But where will the next century get its energy? For Kato, that question raises profound philosophical issues.

"The question is whether we really do need so much consumption of energy. I am opposed to the view that one should accept as granted this ever-increasing consumption of energy."

He admits that the replacement of nuclear power with such alternatives as solar energy probably cannot be done in "an economically feasible way" in the near future. We should "rather try to find out how to live with diminished consumption of energy."

He acknowledges the difficulties facing nations in unilaterally giving up nuclear energy, since such a move could well undercut their "whole competitive ability in the international market." Needed, he says, is an agreement whereby all nations pledge to forgo the use of nuclear power. "If the highly industrialized countries can come to an agreement, no single country will be damaged. That will be the solution and, I would like to stress, the only solution."

"This whole country is getting like a factory," he says, speaking of Japan. "The habitable space is getting narrower and narrower, and all the landscape is being destroyed—natural landscape and historical landscape."

The problem is particularly acute in Japan, where 120 million people crowd onto the fraction of habitable land in a largely mountainous country. "If everything goes on this way," Kato insists, "perhaps [in the 21st century] all developed countries will become like Japan. It's a question of time, if you go on forever."

Kato ranks the problem of pollution and environmental degradation second only to the nuclear threat. He is particularly concerned about the disappearance of forests—taking as his somewhat facetious example the "waste of paper" in the developed countries. "We don't need to publish so much and print so much.

"I am also responsible, because I have published some

books," he adds with a chuckle, "and I don't pretend that these books are absolutely necessary for human beings. So therefore this is a waste of paper."

Beneath his jest, however, is a serious concern. "Only a very tiny proportion of the world's population is wasting paper, namely in the United States and Japan and Europe. Somewhere we have to get the thing down. In Southeast Asia, Canada, and Siberia, the woods are cut down to produce paper to export to the richer nations."

Kato's third major agenda item concerns the "widening gap" between the developed and the developing nations. It is a problem complicated, in his view, by excessive population growth, lack of food and a poor distribution system, and factors of the international economy.

To illustrate the problem, he points to the shipping of surplus wheat from Canada, the United States, and Australia to Africa. He worries that "this kind of aid by the North to the South is in a sense an extreme form of antiprotectionist export—or, to use more brutal words, a kind of dumping." It is extreme, he adds, "because the price is zero."

"If the food price is zero," he explains, "then no domestic industry can compete"—especially in nations where productivity is low and agriculture is hard work. In his view, the temptation in those nations is to quit agriculture and simply depend on aid for survival. That leads to "a vicious circle" where worsening situations demand even more aid.

That is not an argument, he insists, against aid. In fact, he finds the low level of support flowing from North to South "scandalous." The United Nations, he notes, has called for contributions from industrial nations equal to 1 percent of their gross national products (GNP) to help close the North-South gap. But "very few countries in the North are coming up to this 1-percent limit."

Particularly troubling to Kato are the attitudes behind

this lack of aid. Industrial nations are "eager" to spend more than 1 percent of GNP for arms, he says—even though such spending produces only "vague" security against threats that never materialize. Yet the problem in developing nations is immediate. "People are actually dying today," he says, "and not even 1 percent of GNP is spent to save them."

If the problem is not checked, what will be the effect on the industrial world?

Kato foresees, in the 21st century, a threat of what he calls a "Palestinian syndrome"—a volatile, explosive situation in some desperately poor nations, growing out of "the absence of hope for a better tomorrow."

"If today the situation is not very satisfactory but you have hope for tomorrow, you can live. But if you cut off the hope for tomorrow, then the situation will change." That, he says, leads to despair, and "despair produces violence." Such violence—especially in the form of terrorism—cannot be controlled by political oppression, which only makes it worse.

"The heart of the matter is despair and no hope." Insofar as the developed nations cannot provide a sense of hope, they should "expect that a violent reaction will come. I call it the Palestinianization of the world."

"Thinking, in my sense, is the search for truth," says Kato. But in Japan and other developed countries, where a student's entire future seems to hang on the results of a university entrance examination, there is often "no sense of criticism, no habit of thinking thoughts." Instead, truth is viewed as something contained in a textbook, which, if the student is to be successful on the examination, must be absorbed without questioning.

He feels that the Japanese educational system in particular has produced "masses of obedient, reasonable, and gentle people who lack the capacity of thinking on their own." In the past this has produced "an ideal working force for Japanese industry," which was aimed at producing cars. It is not, however, a recipe for success in "innovating the top technology."

Part of the problem, as he sees it, is an overemphasis on competition, which requires conformity. "Competition is only possible when you are doing the same thing. When you are running, everybody's running. How can the Olympic swimming champion and the 100-meter running champion compete? These are two different things. And nobody says which one is better and which one is second-rate."

By the same token, schools should break away from the need to measure everyone by the same standard. They should allow greater diversity. They should not insist that every student compete in the same tests.

"In the 21st century, Japan's future will be in the top exploration of the new fields," says Kato. And that will require broad-minded and original thinkers. "This traditional educational system," he concludes, "is not good for that."

Finally, Kato is interested in the future of the arts—especially poetry, painting, and music. Over the past few centuries, he says, the trend in all the arts has been a steady pushing against the "physioanatomical limitation" of human vision and hearing—by incorporating a progressively wider spectrum of sounds into music, for example, from Bach and Mozart through Wagner and Schoenberg and on to the present.

Where will the arts go in the future?

Kato, with examples from history fresh in his mind, finds it difficult to say. Imagine, he says, standing "at the beginning of the 19th century" and trying to foresee the development of the arts. "Even a genius," he notes, "couldn't anticipate what kinds of objects would be in the Museum of Modern Art in New York. No philosopher was able to anticipate this."

He notes, however, that "the trend must stop sometime." The 21st century, he says, will not see a continuing increase in the range of sounds or colors used—simply because humanity is already "almost to the border" of what it can apprehend.

The result may be a return to more classical forms of artistic expression. "Very likely," he says, "the 21st century will be not a century during which the variety of the materials of artistic expression will increase."

"We can't anticipate," he concludes. "And that is good."

Michael K. Hooker

Metaphysics and Meaningfulness

Looking at his list of publications, you might mistake Michael K. Hooker for an ivory-tower academic philosopher. He is the editor of books on Descartes and Leibniz. His first published essay was titled "In Defense of the Principle for Deductibility of Justification." He later wrote a chapter titled "Deducing and Explaining the Character of Substance" for a book on Spinoza.

In fact, however, the lively chancellor of the University of Maryland's sprawling Baltimore County campus wears his scholarship gracefully—and applies it to everything he sees. "I'm a student of contemporary culture," Hooker confesses. "Not only do I like shopping malls, but I love to pick up fundamentalist preachers on the radio." Why? Because "it tells me so much about society and about people, what they're thinking."

What people are thinking—and how they think—has fascinated Hooker for years. Born in the mountains of southwestern Virginia just after World War II—"my grandfather was a farmer, a common laborer," he says, and "my daddy was a coal miner"—he graduated with highest honors from the University of North Carolina at Chapel Hill in 1969.

After earning a Ph.D. in philosophy at the University of Massachusetts, he taught at Harvard and the Johns Hopkins University in Baltimore, where he moved into academic administration

*in 1977. As president of Bennington College in Vermont from 1982
to 1986, he fought off a serious financial crisis at that private liberal
arts school.*

*His interests in biotechnology (a "strong" field at the Balti-
more County campus, he says) and in Washington-based politics led
him back to Baltimore, where he hopes to see his campus "become
the model university of the 21st century." Married in 1968, he has a
six-year-old daughter.*

Baltimore, Maryland

On the one hand, the future according to Michael Hooker is
an intriguing place. "You will walk into a McDonald's," he
says, "and you will say to a very friendly-looking machine,
'I'd like a Big Mac, please, and I'd like it cooked to order. I'd
like it medium rare, and hold the mayonnaise.'

"The machine will say to you in a very pleasing voice,
'That will be $1.59. Would you like anything to drink?' And
you say, 'Oh, yes, I'd like a Diet Coke.' And the machine
says, 'That will be $2.35.'

"You deposit your money in any kind of denomina-
tion, or you can write it a check. Or probably you'll just
speak in a credit-card code. . . . And by the time it has
finished recording the information, your cooked-to-order
Big Mac, microwaved, will be delivered out the slot, and
you'll say, 'Thank you,' and the machine will say, 'Thank
you,' in a very pleasant voice, and you'll go away.

"That's in ten years. In twenty years, the machine will
recognize your voice. . . ."

Slipping off his black loafers and lounging back in an
upholstered chair in his tenth-floor office, Hooker expands
on his vision, which finally reaches beyond high-tech into
what he calls "metaphysics."

It will be, he says, a world of laser-guided cars that
locate parking places by satellite positioning, of voice-

activated home computers with access to "every piece of unclassified information in the world."

By the middle of the next century, it may even be a world in which biotechnology will have retarded aging, engineered away most genetically based diseases, and provided means for the human body to regenerate severed limbs and broken teeth. Pollution may well be solved, as one industry's pollutants become another's feedstocks; agricultural sufficiency may well arise from new fast-growing, disease-resistant strains of plants; and energy sufficiency may well come about through biologically enhanced methods of fossil-fuel recovery and biomass conversions of plant material into fuels.

On the other hand, it will be a world that sobers us with an entirely new order of problems, all based on one question: What will we do with our leisure time?

"Throughout human history," says Hooker, "most of humanity's time has been occupied with survival." When the basic survival questions are answered—when 21st-century technology has provided all the necessities of food and shelter—what will people do all day?

Hooker is far more interested in that question than in the futurist particulars of technological progress. He can, of course, spin out any number of gee-whiz scenarios, some of which, he freely admits, are more probable than others. But what most concerns him is the serious impact of these changes on the human heart and soul—and the unwillingness, so far, of social and political thinkers to plan for such changes.

"I foresee a kind of growing intellectual and cultural and ethical anomie," he says, drawing on his philosopher's training for a Greek word meaning *rootlessness* or *lack of purpose.* He defines it as "a condition where people have nothing to live for, nothing to commit their lives to, no sense of meaningful activity in their lives, because they have no sense of meaningfulness in their lives."

Part of the problem, says Hooker, arises as two modern trends begin to come together. One is the shift, already well under way in America, toward a two-track service economy consisting of highly paid managers and professionals and low-skilled, low-wage employees. The other is the increasing use of robotics to replace these low-skilled workers with machines.

"I'm not worried that service workers won't be fed and clothed. They will be. But they won't be service workers anymore. They will be idle. What will they do with their lives? And what in the world could we be doing now to prepare for that day?"

The day, in fact, may not be far off.

Hooker already sees signs of this anomie in the segment of society that, as an educator, he knows best: the youth culture. He sees it in the prevalence of drug use and in the increases in teen suicide. He also sees it in such physical symbols as the suburban shopping mall.

"I'm a kind of student of the suburban shopping mall. They fascinate me. When I go to a strange city on business, if I have an evening free and I have a rental car, sometimes I go to a suburban shopping mall just to absorb the flavor."

What he finds in malls across the country is not difference but sameness. And what worries him—especially among the youth who wander through the malls—is "an emptiness in their eyes—an emptiness that reflects, I think, an emptiness in their lives."

Hooker sees in the mall a symbol of a central shift in society. "When I was a kid," he recalls, "I worked. I came home; I worked after school. I worked weekends—had a part-time job, and if I wasn't at my part-time job, I was mowing the lawn or taking out the garbage or doing something around the house. I was occupied.

"Kids today don't have that necessity of occupation. So an emptiness creeps in. That doesn't mean that my life was more meaningful than their lives. It's just that I had activity to fill it, so I didn't have time to dwell on the meaninglessness of my life, if you will."

What worries him today is that young people do not have the mental means to come to terms with either the meaningfulness or the meaninglessness of their lives.

"Dwelling on the meaninglessness of your life," he says with the philosopher's conviction of the value of thought, "is a meaningful activity. What I'm concerned about is the people who *don't* dwell on the meaninglessness of their lives, or the meaningfulness of it—who just pursue mindless entertainment. The shopping mall is a contemporary opium. Half of the kids there are stoned anyway, but the other half are stoned by the mall. The mall provides a kind of transfixing environment that takes their mind off of whatever their issues are. They walk around—you look in their eyes, and there's nobody home."

Is there an answer? Hooker, no pessimist, is convinced that there is, and that it lies not simply in more and better technology but in what he calls "metaphysics."

In a paper delivered in 1985 at the University of New Hampshire for a conference on universities in the 21st century, Hooker raised the issue of the university's role in preparing students for a changing world.

"The real challenge," he told his colleagues, "is to provide a metaphysics that adequately subtends our changing conception of the universe and our place in it, and our conception of the nature of life and the nature of persons. While these matters are inextricably linked to religion, they will be inescapable for universities in the next century."

Expanding on that point, Hooker emphasizes that "we need to think about metaphysics. We need to confront questions on a broad scale that we have never confronted before—such as 'What makes life worth living? What makes it meaningful? What is its human purpose?' And these are, of course, religious questions."

Religious, but not necessarily fundamentalist. Hooker, who grew up with what he calls the "Bible-thumping" fundamentalism of rural Virginia, still loves to listen to fundamentalist preachers on the radio, because "it tells me so much" about what people are thinking. And he lauds what he calls "the return to a recognition of a sense of values" in much of the preaching.

But he notes that the new popularity of fundamentalism can be explained in part by the fact that "it frames issues in black and white" and thereby "removes the necessity for thinking, for reasoning—and people will do anything to avoid the pain of having to think for themselves."

Running like an obbligato throughout the interview, in fact, is Hooker's insistence on "the necessity for thinking." There are, he notes, "few blacks and whites in the world. One of the problems that we have in society, when dealing with ethical issues in areas like euthanasia, medical ethics, abortion, etc., is that people are not capable of dealing with the complexity of real-world issues. They want things to be black and white. People don't like ambiguity."

The result, Hooker believes, is a widespread failure of truth telling in public life, since many issues are inherently ambiguous. Politicians "need to acknowledge that questions are not as simple as they are framed to be in the media and in the press."

And that leads him to one of the major items on the 21st century's agenda: the reform of journalism, which he says has "an incredibily powerful influence over people." While he points the most accusatory finger at television news—which he calls "pernicious" because it "frames everything in terms of the good guys and the bad guys"—he is also exercised over print journalism.

"As an educator, as a public person, I have a responsibility to try to get the media to be more responsible . . . in acknowledging that issues are not framed in black and white—that everything is vastly more complicated than we want to believe that it is."

He is in fact calling for a wholesale reform of journalism.

"If people at the everyday, man-on-the-street level are going to come to understand and appreciate and grapple with the uncertainty and the ambiguity of the questions of life, it is going to come about in part because journalists begin to acknowledge what they all know: namely, that the world is not as simple as we tend to portray it to be."

How can a university respond to that need to "grapple with the uncertainty"?

Despite Hooker's fascination with technology and the sciences, his ideal curriculum leans strongly in another direction.

"I'd educate everybody in the humanities—literature, philosophy, poetry." Why? Because "they tell the truth."

The history of literature, he explains, is "the history of pointing out that the world is not as simple as it seems, that life is filled with ambiguity and uncertainty, that we deceive ourselves right and left. Literature tells the truth. And if it doesn't tell the truth it's not literature, it's propaganda or something else."

Does that lead him to worry about literacy? Yes, but not—fittingly—in a black-and-white way.

"You don't have to be literate to be capable of thinking," he says. "Back in the mountains where I grew up in the southwestern part of Virginia, I knew a lot of people who couldn't read and write but were very smart and could teach me a great deal.

"We could have a society of illiterate people who think. The reason for literacy is that it adds meaningfulness to people's lives."

How? Here, even the philosopher is at a loss for words. "Reading," he says, "is an encounter with the word." And "the word," he explains, "is a reified entity that has significance in and of itself, quite apart from what it signifies."

Then, with an almost embarrassed wave of the hand, Hooker apologizes for slipping into the jargon of philosophy.

"There's no way to express that, other than in the airy-fairy terms that I just did. But part of what makes us human is that we have words available to us."

Reasonable Discourse

II

People are losing the art of reasonable discourse.

—Norman Cousins

Norman Cousins

Barbara W. Tuchman

Paul Johnson

Hanna H. Gray

Amitai Etzioni

Norman Cousins

Creating Institutions

At the end of the previous section, Michael Hooker noted that the philosopher is constantly encountering "the word" in its most abstract manifestations. The five voices in this section—those of Norman Cousins, Barbara Tuchman, Paul Johnson, Hanna Gray, and Amitai Etzioni—take a somewhat different approach to their words. As journalists, historians, and social scientists, they speak from the crossroads where the abstract comes face to face with the need to communicate historical insights to a wide and diverse audience.

Not surprisingly, their assessments of the future stand solidly on the past. If they share one belief, it is perhaps George Santayana's dictum that "those who cannot remember the past are condemned to repeat it." Shaping, composing, and interpreting the world, they use words as tools: Norman Cousins might well be speaking for them all when he says, "As far back as I can remember, I've been interested in print."

Cousins, who begins this section, was born in New Jersey and attended Teachers College, Columbia University. After working as a journalist for several years, he joined the faltering Saturday Review *in 1940 as executive editor. Over the next thirty-six years he built it into a widely respected weekly with a circulation of nearly half a million.*

Campaigning tirelessly for such humanitarian causes as world

*government, disarmament, and peace, he wrote editorials from air-
plane seats, acted as unofficial ambassador for President John F.
Kennedy in negotiating the nuclear test ban treaty, and found time to
write hundreds of essays and more than a dozen books.* When the
Saturday Review *folded in 1982, Cousins wrote sadly, "people
are losing the art of reasonable discourse."*

*Struck with a paralyzing disease in the mid-sixties, Cousins
healed himself largely through what he called "the salutary emotions"—later writing a book,* Anatomy of an Illness, *about his
healing. Now, as an adjunct professor in the School of Medicine at
University of California in Los Angeles, he gives his attention to
what he calls "the medical humanities," working to "mobilize the
human being's resources—spiritual, physical, biological—in order
to get a good [healing] result."*

Beverly Hills, California

"The big news of the 21st century," says Norman Cousins,
"will be that the world *as a whole* has to be managed, and not
just its parts."

If a single word could be found to characterize Mr.
Cousins's thinking, it might well be *wholeness.* He makes it
his business to stand back, take the broad view, and weave
the threads of culture, humanities, medicine, public policy,
and international affairs into a single tapestry.

And that, as he sees it, is just what the world must do as
it rolls toward the 21st century.

"The division of the human species into national tribes
has outlived its usefulness," he said in the course of a two-
hour interview in his book-lined hilltop home. The result has
brought to the fore "the most important issue of our time,"
which he defines as the need to recognize that the entire
world is "a unit with clearly identifiable problems pertaining
to the whole."

What are those problems? With the assurance of a man
who has thought about them deeply, Cousins ticks off four:

- Weapons that can "pulverize the human species"
- Environmental deterioration so severe as to "threaten the
  natural balances that are necessary to sustain life"
- World hunger
- World squalor.

These, he hastens to add, are not new problems. But they
exist, nowadays, in a "form so heightened that people don't
want to think about them."

It's a sobering list. But a further challenge—the unwillingness of humanity even to "think about" these problems—
is clearly Cousins's overarching concern. Even what he calls
the "saturation of tension" produced by the presence of
weapons of mass destruction—the issue that many thinkers
place at the top of the 21st century's agenda—is not for
Cousins the most pressing one.

"The No. 1 problem in the world," he concludes, "is
not the presence of all this destructive weaponry, or the emphasis on it and the organizations attached to it. That's the
No. 2 problem. The No. 1 problem is the inability to recognize the No. 2 problem."

And what occupies Cousins's attention these days is not
so much the specific problems facing the world, serious
though they are, as the lack of structures through which to
deal with them. It is this failure—the inadequacy of the
world's social and political institutions—to which he returns
again and again throughout the conversation.

"The institutions that we have tend to pull us back
rather than enable us to cope with those problems." The
reason: "Those institutions not only are incapable of meeting
the need but actually intensify the need."

As he talks, examples emerge. Drawing from his latest

book, *The Pathology of Power,* he calls attention to the influence exercised over defense-spending decisions by the nation's powerful manufacturing interests—noting, in this context, President Eisenhower's warnings concerning America's military-industrial complex. "The threat to American security today," Cousins notes, "is represented not so much by an outside enemy as by the fact that decision making with respect to national security and the programs connected to it is being carried out by people who have no [financial] stake in peace."

As in the United States, so also abroad. "The principal threat to the health of the world's peoples today," he says, figuratively donning his medical-research hat, "is represented not by cancer but by the foreign policies of their governments. The failure of those foreign policies will be translated into more death and disease [if there is nuclear war] than all our medical institutions combined can possibly take on."

Yet even these problems, precisely defined as they are, take a back seat to what Cousins sees as larger instances of institutional breakdown—related, in general, to the inadequacy of the institution of national government itself.

This problem, for Cousins, shows up in the United States in one clear manifestation: the fact that it is "difficult to get the attention of government for anything that has a long-range nature."

"If you talk to a congressman about something that will surface more than two years from now, a glaze comes over his eyes," says Cousins, who has had plenty of opportunity to do that sort of talking. "The term of office, unfortunately, tends to dictate the readiness of officeholders to consider problems."

"The mainframe of American society," he concludes, is "not constructed to look at or deal with long-term issues."

But the real difficulty, in his view, lies in the very presence of national governments themselves and in the failure of nations to adopt a form of world government.

That, as Cousins well knows, is a controversial position to take—especially in a nation that, over the past few years, has been experiencing a resurgence of patriotism. So he is at pains to describe his position, and its historical roots, in some detail.

Nations, in his view, came into being in a natural evolution away from tribes and, later, from city-states. "The purpose of the nation was to protect the lives, values, and the cultures" of its citizens.

Today, however, "no nation is able any longer to meet those purposes"—no longer capable, for example, of "protecting its people from war or in war. And yet the nation still regards war as its ultimate challenge and function. And in the very act of attempting to meet the needs of war, paradoxically, we get closer to it, because the instruments of war reach a point where you don't want to be hit first." The result, in Cousins's view, is a spiraling arms race that ignores the real needs of national security.

"So we move into the 21st century, where the entire human race has all the requirements of a tribe. Geographically, it's in a compressed area. Sociologically and economically, it has to interact—and there are aspects not only of interaction but of interdependence that have to be addressed. But it lacks the adequate institutions to make the unit workable and viable."

All of which could sound like a recipe for profound pessimism. But Cousins, a patient listener whose manner tends toward the formal and whose humor is quiet and reserved, is no pessimist. "Let me plagiarize myself," he says with a smile, referring to the voluminous writing he has done over his long career, "and say that I really don't know enough to be a pessimist." Admitting to grave doubts about existing institutions, he nevertheless says that "I'm optimistic about the intangibles that could be converted into assets or answers."

What's the basis of his optimism? "Creating institutions has always been a standard business of the human species," Cousins observes. All that means is that "you recognize that a form has to be provided, competence has to be created, responsibilities have to be fixed, and mechanisms for repair have to be brought into being. That's all a government is. But there are different forms of government, of course. The progress of the people depends on what form of government is created"—or, in other words, on "how they organize their collective life."

For Cousins, the obvious solution lies in creating supranational institutions constituting a form of world federal government.

What about the United Nations as a model? While praising some of its agencies, Cousins is well aware of the U.N.'s limitations. "The United Nations, like the Articles of Confederation [of the American colonies] from 1783 to 1787, is a reflection of an existing situation rather than an effort to transcend the situation."

The articles didn't last. They proved, in Cousins's view, inadequate to the task and were superseded by a constitution calling on the separate states to surrender some autonomy for the sake of a stronger whole.

The result: the creation of the United States, which Cousins calls "the most spectacular example of a nation that was *designed,* designed to meet a certain purpose." The parallel to today's world, he says, "is obvious, both philosophically and politically."

"The choices, it seems to me, are whether this gravitational pull, this historical pull toward a world unit, will produce a world totalitarian society, à la George Orwell, where the natural forces to create the whole will be brought about and governed by force. Or will the human intelligence be brought to bear on the problem in order to create a society of the whole which will make progress possible in some degree of human development and decency?"

Needed, he feels, is the will to reinvent the way humanity thinks. "We move into the 21st century without the philosophy or the sociology or the politics that can keep the species going."

Then must the process of reform begin with individuals? Cousins puts great faith in education. "If governments by themselves are part of the problem instead of part of the answer," he says, then "education becomes the only means by which you can get people to a point where they make the demand for reform."

But time, he feels, is not on humanity's side—and education takes time. "We can't wait for a regeneration of the heart of man before we can meet the world problems. I think that we have to assume that it's the imperfections that represent the problem. And we don't have to become perfect before we deal with those imperfections."

How, then, will progress come about? The metaphor he finds most helpful—the metaphor of healing—arises from his own researches and his own healings, described in detail in two of his books. These have convinced him that "the body moves down the path of its expectations. There are vast psychological factors at work in health, illness, and the treatment of illness. And these have to be respected." He concludes that "the healing system is tied to the belief system."

"I think, in the 21st century, we're going to learn a great deal more about . . . the human healing system and how to tend to it, nurture it, and evoke it, rather than just to try to repair it."

And it is here, finally, that the medical professor and

the global thinker become one. "The most neglected field of medicine has to do with the knowledge of the human healing system, which is very real. And the same thing is true of nations, which is that the healing capabilities of nations are not well understood, but they're real nonetheless. And both with respect to the ability of the individual to heal and with respect to the nation to heal, we have ample opportunity to enlist some of our finest minds.

"I think that throughout the entire world there's a growing sense of human community. There's a growing awareness of a common destiny and common needs.

"I can't conceive of any problem that the human mind can define that it can't also solve. I think that what makes the human race unique is its ability to do something for the first time. And for the first time we're called upon to meet a threat to the survival of the species."

Barbara W. Tuchman

An Age of Disruption

*"I'm not trying to teach anything; I never wanted to be a teacher,"
says Barbara W. Tuchman, who is probably America's best-known
contemporary historian. "I am a seeker of the small facts, not the big
Explanation," she has written, "a narrator, not a philosopher."*

*Judging from the popularity of her work, thousands of readers
feel she has succeeded.* The Guns of August *(1962) and* Stilwell
and the American Experience in China *(1971) won Pulitzer
prizes.* More recently, A Distant Mirror *(1978) and* The March
of Folly *(1984) have been highly praised. Her goal, she has written, is "to write history so as to enthrall the reader and to make the
subject as captivating and exciting to him as it is to me."*

*Born Barbara Wertheim, daughter of an influential interna-
tional banker and publisher in New York City, she graduated from
Radcliffe College in 1933, beginning her writing career as an editorial assistant and writer with* The Nation *magazine in 1935. She
later served as United States correspondent for the British journal*
New Statesman and Nation. *Her first book,* The Lost British
Policy: Britain and Spain Since 1700, *was published in London
in 1938.*

Widespread recognition came with The Zimmerman Tele-
gram *in 1958 and its condensed version in* Reader's Digest *the
following year. Her essays have since appeared in* The New Re-

public, The Atlantic, Esquire, Foreign Affairs, The Christian Science Monitor, *and other publications.*

Tuchman counts her early reading of fiction—especially the tales of Sir Arthur Conan Doyle and the historical novels of Alexandre Dumas—as a strong influence on her career. But she distinguishes sharply between history and fiction. "I do not invent anything, even the weather," she told an audience at Radcliffe in 1963. "Leaving things out because they do not fit is writing fiction, not history."

Cos Cob, Connecticut

She's a student of kings and popes and presidents, and a public figure in her own right. But most of Barbara Tuchman's real work—the writing that brings history alive for thousands of readers—happens in the privacy of her home.

In her friendly manner she offers a visitor her "husband's favorite chair." She seats herself at her cluttered desk next to a wall of color snapshots of grandchildren and fifty-year-old family black-and-whites.

The only cleared space on her desk, however, is occupied by the manuscript of her latest book, dealing with the American Revolution. Scattered about are the periodicals that reveal her eclectic interests: *Foreign Affairs, Daedalus,* the *Harvard Library Bulletin, Art & Antiques.* Among the photos is one of then-President Carter, book in hand, at an outdoor table with Vice-President Mondale. "To Barbara," it says in Mr. Mondale's scrawl, "We begin every meeting by reading from Tuchman."

Not surprisingly, Tuchman's agenda for the 21st century seems to blend her public and personal interests. It includes such prominent topics as nuclear war and the environment. But it puts its leading emphasis on morality. Above all, it is an agenda firmly rooted in her understanding of history.

Tuchman begins the discussion with the issue of nuclear weaponry—although that is not in the No. 1 spot on her agenda.

"I wouldn't put it at the top because, although I haven't got much trust in humanity's common sense, I just somehow don't see it all exploding," she says. "I can't say why. I suppose it's only because it just seems too extreme to happen. All these articles that tell you we're on the brink of exploding, blowing up the world and so forth, I should take seriously, but I don't, really. Maybe because I'm just unable to conceive of it."

In her own way, however, she has tried to "conceive of it" in *A Distant Mirror,* her widely read book on 14th-century Europe.

"I was looking for a model or an example of what happened to society in a major lethal disaster," she says. The disaster was the Black Death, a plague whose recurrent cycles so ravaged Europe that one-third of the population died.

"That seemed to me the most extreme disaster that had happened in the course of history. I chose that, the Black Death, as a model of what might happen from a nuclear explosion.

"But what I found was that the 14th century had so many disasters and violences that you couldn't isolate or determine exactly which trouble came from the plague. And, in fact, I came to the conclusion that the various troubles did not all necessarily come from the plague by any means."

She chose the 14th century as a "mirror" for the 20th century, she says, "because it was so distinctly an age where everything was disappearing, everything that people believed in."

If she were a 21st-century historian looking back at the present day, how would she characterize it?

"I would call it an Age of Disruption."

We live, she explains, "in an age where things seem to have gotten beyond control." The weapons race, for example, is subject to "our relations with the Soviet Union"—which, like many elusive problems, "keeps on getting away from us."

More important, in her view, is the disruption of man's relation with the environment. "This loss or deterioration of the natural world," she says, "is probably the number one problem—because I think it's already more with us than is the nuclear."

A great lover of nature—as is evident from the well-cared-for acres of her southern Connecticut estate—she is concerned about "the loss of the products of the natural world that we live by: trees, water, the stripping of forests and damming of rivers, the poisoning of the air, the loss of forests in the tropical world."

"All these things are raising real dangers."

Yet even the environmental issue is superseded in significance by another. "My own concern is something else," she says, something she describes as "the real deterioration in public morality."

With the writer's penchant for specifics, she points to current events. She has been deeply disturbed by revelations that National Aeronautics and Space Administration officials knew about problems with shuttle booster-rocket seals long before launching *Challenger* in January 1986. The fact of their "knowing that there was danger and going on with the program without rectifying the troubles," she says, is "so shocking that you can't quite absorb it."

"That's only one small example of a much larger decline in public morality," she adds, which "seems to me to pervade many fields of current life." She also points to "cheating on the stock market" and, in the political realm, the "sale of influence" and the corruption of elected officials.

Particularly damaging to public morality, she feels, is the current electoral process. "I see as a dangerous development the emphasis on . . . fund raising." Campaigns are no longer based on "the beliefs or functions of the person" but rather on "what kind of artificial image the candidate can project through professional fund raisers, whose effectiveness is determined entirely by their skill in certain methods rather than by the quality of the person they're selling.

"I think this is lowering the quality factor—if we can say that, since it's never been very high—of the people we're engaging in government. And that's serious, because we depend for common sense and rational policy on the kinds of people we put in office."

Where does the problem come from? It's the result, she says, of "the grip of status and power."

"Everybody who gets into government wants to exert power and hold onto it. When they see things happening that are clearly signs of failure, they don't ring a bell . . . because they're afraid of losing their position. They don't want to tell the boss—whether it's Chiang Kai-shek or Reagan or Nixon or whoever it is—what he doesn't want to hear."

"You know," she muses, "I say to myself, 'If we could change the rewards—if, instead of status and power, people got their reward in life through some other satisfaction.' But I don't think that's possible, either, because what does move people to really energetic action is doing something for themselves." In the Middle Ages, she notes, "they used to call it greed."

The problem of public morality, for Tuchman, is mirrored in private morality. The two "go hand in hand," because when "this sinking of public morality" appears "so normal" to the citizenry, "they naturally apply it to themselves" and begin to behave the same way.

But hasn't that always been so? Drawing from her rich

historical store, she casts her mind back over Restoration England, the poverty and squalor depicted in Hogarth's drawings, and the early years of the Industrial Revolution. "I suppose there have always been times when people have acted immorally," she concedes. What is new is "the extent of *public* immorality making itself so obvious to the average citizen."

And that, for Tuchman, is the ultimate disruption. "When I speak of disruption, I mean a period when we've lost belief in certain kinds of moral understanding of good and bad. I think that has left many people feeling uneasy, because . . . they don't know how to behave, they don't know what's right and what's wrong."

Are there obvious culprits? She points at popular journalism and television entertainment—which, she says, are "really pretty deadly on any level of taste or any level of ethics." She then extends the list to include contemporary fiction.

In the "average novel of the present, the source of tension or drama is always in some very aberrant situation—you know, somebody's committing incest, or trying to murder his mother, or he's insane, or he's alcoholic, or whatever. . . . There's no sense in the author of viewing it as—well, I don't want to say an immoral situation, but in a way I do. He's got no sense of why he's telling it except for the degree of shock and excitement that he can introduce.

"I suppose that the absence of admirable models has an effect on all of this—and the examples of the *unadmirable* being the success stories." She especially faults journalism for "emphasizing the shock value of wrong and of disaster and morbidity."

"I think journalism has to try and make good actions . . . more newsworthy," she says. "When you see some group that has cleaned up its local river and brought the salmon back, or a family that has brought up six sons on no kind of income, all of whom turn out to be effective citizens—that sort of thing can be made more attractive to the public."

If admirable models are missing, however, that may be because of the absence of what she calls "religion as a major force in everyday life."

"I don't know how much less people really relate to religion or churchgoing [these days]," she concedes, "because . . . I've never been a religious person. But I do think that there's a kind of absence of common understanding, particularly with the young as they grow up, of what's good behavior and bad behavior, and what's right and what's wrong. That is disappearing."

That ability to distinguish good from bad is something Tuchman obviously practices herself, even in the minutiae of her daily life. When she was buying presents for her infant grandchildren, she says, "I always used to make an effort to get toys that were not these horrid, primary, plastic colors . . . but only to buy toys that I thought were pretty or attractive—so that the children wouldn't get used to ugly things.

"You know, if the growing population is given nothing but the shoddy and the artificial and the false, they're going to have more and more difficulty in discerning the difference between good and bad."

But this "growing population" of children, she fears, is not being taught how to "get hold of their own lives." She admits that getting hold of life is not always easy—especially for women. The issue of "women's place in society" is "something that still has to be solved and worked through" in the future. She says she has little faith in "the solution of the new woman" or in "feminist" approaches. "Unless women have part-time work, which nobody's satisfied with, or a remarkably cooperative husband, something has to give."

How has Tuchman managed to "get hold" of her own life?

"I never thought I was particularly smart," she says with a self-deprecating laugh. But "over my years I've used myself. I think people don't do that enough. They let things happen to them. That's no way to learn."

Is that sense of passivity related to the influence of television?

"I don't know whether television's *responsible* or whether it's *responding,*" she says. She dismisses the excuse for poor programming given by television executives who say they are simply giving the audience what it wants. "There's a missing quality of responsibility there," she asserts.

Asked whether, in an Age of Disruption, she can identify any single thing most needed in the next century, she replies without hesitation.

"Probably personal responsibility," she says, explaining that she means "taking responsibility for your behavior and your expenditures and your actions, and not forever supposing that society must forgive you because it's not your fault."

Paul Johnson

Classical Values for Modern Times

"History is the most important thing to learn," says British author Paul Johnson. "It's more important than almost any other discipline if you're involved in high-level decisions."

In his voluminous writings, Johnson practices what he preaches. In Modern Times: The World from the Twenties to the Eighties *(1983), he takes a comprehensive, sweeping, and often iconoclastic look at the 20th century. In* A History of the Jews *(1987), he surveys the development of the Jewish people from antiquity to the present.*

In more than a dozen earlier books, he has examined subjects ranging from the Suez war to Pope John XXIII, from the history of Christianity to British castles.

Educated at Stonyhurst and at Magdalen College, Oxford, Johnson joined the editorial staff of the left-wing New Statesman *magazine in 1955, becoming editor in 1965.*

Then, in a political volte-face that stunned his contemporaries, he took up the conservative cause, threw his support behind British Prime Minister Margaret Thatcher's government, and became a columnist for the right-wing Spectator *magazine—in whose pages he noted that "most considerable thinkers in Britain now incline to the Right of the political spectrum." A frequent lecturer, he often discusses the future from a historical perspective.*

"It wouldn't at all surprise me," warns author and columnist Paul Johnson, "if the first decade, or at any rate the second decade, of the 21st century is a decade of illusions—grand expectations, all kinds of rosy dreams."

The reason? Settling into an easy chair in his third-floor London *pied-à-terre,* Johnson notes that two trends now in the making will by then have peaked. One involves demographics, the other, technology.

The demographic trend, says Johnson, will bring into positions of authority a group of leaders for whom the lessons of the recent past will be no more than "ancient history." These lessons, he explains, arise from a study of the past three decades.

First came what he calls an earlier Decade of Illusions in the 1960s, when Western nations imagined that they could "increase state spending, welfare spending, defense spending, all kinds of investment, and at the same time increase personal spending almost indefinitely—with full employment, too.

"Then in the 1970s came the Decade of Disillusionment," marked by the end of the postwar economic boom, the energy crisis, and the "particular crisis of government and confidence in the United States" known as Watergate.

With the 1980s, he says, came "the Decade of Realism," during which Margaret Thatcher's government in Britain and Ronald Reagan's administration in the United States encouraged a return to "old-fashioned virtues."

The net effect of these three decades, according to Johnson, has been salutary. "If you are old enough today to remember how very unpleasant hyperinflation was in the '70s," he says, "it's unlikely that you will ever fall for policies that tend to induce very high rates of inflation." People now in their twenties, he says, share those memories. And they will be in leadership positions in the 1990s.

What concerns Johnson, however, is "the generation after that—the generation that will take over and occupy important positions between the year 2000 and the year 2020—because they won't have had this experience."

At about the time they come into leadership positions, the second trend will make itself felt: the marriage of electronic communications and biotechnology.

Through biotechnology, says Johnson, "it will be possible to produce materials on which the number of minicircuits will be multiplied almost indefinitely." The result, he says, will be a generation of machines having "more of the characteristics and flexibility of the human mind" and able to "analyze things very closely and carefully and take decisions accordingly."

Those developments, he concludes, will coincide with the coming to power of "the new generation that doesn't know the experience of the 1970s" and therefore has "the kind of idealistic illusions that will fit in rather well with the period of seemingly indefinite expansion" ushered in by the new electronic revolution. The result, he warns, could be a repetition of "the sort of mistakes that were made in the '60s."

As these developments arrive, they will in turn be shaped by the political landscape of the 21st century. In a brief *tour d'horizon*, Johnson charts that landscape:

Japan Johnson says Japan is poised to enter its "really creative period." Until now, the Japanese have "principally been taking developments they've inherited from the West and improving them." In the future, he foresees them increasingly "leading in technology."

Yet Japan remains, for Johnson, an "anomaly." Historically, he explains, the development of economic leadership by an emerging nation has "inevitably and quite quickly been followed by an increase in political and military power."

But Japan, although its economy is second only to that of the United States, has "very little political power, virtually no military power, and an apparent disinclination to exercise either." Johnson predicts that in the 21st century, it will be "almost inevitable" that Japan will "reemerge as a major political and military power."

United States   "The most important thing that the first quarter of the 21st century will decide is whether the United States is in a pattern of decline or not."

His hunch, he says, is that it is not, since the United States has "enormous physical, territorial, and psychological resources" and has proved itself to be "capable of periodic renewals and recharging of energy."

America, he notes, is "the best-known and the least-known country in the world." Although Europeans think they know it well through movies, television, and periodic visits to its major cities, "it's a very different country, with all kinds of things that we simply don't possess over here [in Europe] and with an absence of certain hang-ups.

"My guess is that America will survive as a major power" in the 21st century, and will remain "the anchorman of the West for the foreseeable future."

Western Europe   Since 1945, "Europe has had a marvelous quarter-century." Yet it remains "a sleeping princess." Having emerged from "a terrible period" of wars earlier in this century, Western Europe now enjoys "a far higher living standard than it ever had in the whole of its history. And for the first time every single country in Western Europe is a democracy."

Like Japan, however, Europe remains an anomaly: Economically strong, it lacks commensurate military might and international influence. "It has a much greater collective economy than the Soviet Union," Johnson notes. "Yet it always has to rely upon the United States for its basic strategic defense." The question for the 21st century is whether this anomaly is "going to be corrected."

What Europe most needs, he says, is "a new literary, artistic stimulus," which he expects will develop during the first decades of the 21st century.

Looking back at the Europe of Dante, Shakespeare, and Goethe, he notes that "it is the poets, the dramatists, the great writers, who provide the big ideas which later the statesmen and the generals, as it were, put into practice.

"Who is going to be the next European writer who will kiss the sleeping princess and awaken her?" he asks.

Asia If, as Johnson foresees, Japan attains new political and military power, then a major question facing the 21st century will be "the China-Japan relationship." Will it be, he asks, one of enmity or one of partnership? If a partnership, "which will be the senior partner? Or could they achieve a partnership of equality?"

Equality would be "the most desirable solution." Given the size of China and the economic strength of Japan, such a partnership "would of course create the most important economic unit by far in the world."

Also very much in the Asian picture, however, is India—"a rather ramshackle social-democratic, parliamentary democracy, which has done very much better than one might have expected." He says India has "a lot of weaknesses." But he adds that "it has a kind of staying power which one would not have predicted"—and which he attributes, in part, to its British heritage. He expects, in the 21st century, that living standards in India will rise faster than those in China—largely because India benefits from a partially free market economy.

Middle East Johnson says the Arab world "missed its great opportunity" with the oil boom. "They could have transformed themselves. They could have brought their thinking into modern times: They could have created an industrial economy, and they failed to do it.

"I would guess that in the 21st century the Arab world will be less important than it has been." He sees plenty of promise, however, for two countries: Turkey, which he expects to have "a good century in the 21st century," and Iran, which will be "a very impressive country" when it "gets rid of the fanatics."

Africa Among the fity-odd nations that make up this continent, he says, most have "gone downhill" in the last twenty-five years—making Africa "a very sad case." The problem: excessive population growth, which he says always follows a "predictable pattern."

"When you go through these terrific population surges, it always means a great deal of either imperialism or of political instability, revolution, and so on." Europe and Asia passed through large population surges—with their attendant instabilities—several decades ago.

More recently, Latin America passed the peak of the surge—with the exception of Central America, where population growth is still a challenge.

But he says Africa is just entering its population surge. "There's going to be a great deal more growth and instability over the next thirty or forty years," he warns.

Latin America "People have been predicting a tremendous future for Latin America since the 16th century, and it's never actually happened." For him, the most likely success story is Brazil, which has "an extraordinarily mixed, multiracial society" with "huge minorities" from Europe and Japan. Already, "there are large areas of the country where things are going well," leading him to think Brazil could become "a major economic power in the 21st century."

Soviet Union Historically, says Johnson, the Russian people have proved themselves to be "enormously conservative." Today the Soviet regime "benefits from the instinctive feeling among the Russian people that this is the regime that they've always had, as it were, and it oughtn't to be changed."

Can the Soviet Union undergo major reforms? Johnson does not think so. "The most important single factor about the regime is the absolute monopoly of power exercised by the Communist Party. Until you change that monopoly, you can't have structural reform of any consequence. And *if* you change that monopoly, I don't believe the regime as a whole can survive."

He sees, instead, "a long period of stagnation for the Soviet Union" during which there could be "breakaways in Eastern Europe that the Soviets are unable or lack the will to prevent."

Standing back from the world he has just sketched, Johnson sees little likelihood that the present "nuclear deadlock" will be changed. History teaches that "you never actually get effective disarmament agreements unless the basic political obstacles, which have made the powers arm in the first place, are removed."

"I think if we could solve our ideological and political differences, there wouldn't be much trouble about a disarmament treaty. But to get the second without the first, I'm afraid, just doesn't work in practice."

Johnson also expresses little concern about the environment. "I think this is a 20th-century problem that we're in the process of solving." He adds, "I don't see it as a major 21st-century problem at all."

High on his agenda, however, stands the question of education.

"One of the things we've got to do in the 21st century is to rethink the whole ideology of education. I think we're going to have a lot of opportunities in the 21st century to spend the profits of an expanding world economy on desirable leisure and cultural ends. And no one has yet produced, to my mind, a rational philosophy as to how those ends should be pursued.

"Perhaps the most important thing that will happen in the 21st century," he concludes, "is a rebirth of classical cultural values and civilization—after a century of frenzied experiment that hasn't really produced very much."

Hanna H. Gray

Demography as Destiny

When Hanna H. Gray accepted her present position as president of the University of Chicago in 1978, she took up what Newsweek *magazine described as "the most prestigious academic post ever held by a woman."*

Setting "first woman" records, however, was nothing new to Gray: She was the first woman to be dean of arts and sciences at Northwestern University (1972–1974), and the first woman provost of Yale University (1974–1978).

Born into a distinguished academic family in Heidelberg, Germany, she was raised in New Haven, Connecticut, where her father had accepted a post at Yale after leaving Germany because of his opposition to the Nazis. She once recalled being brought up "under all kinds of German theories" that included having no pillows, no white bread, and only two radio programs a week. A great fan of such entertainers as Edgar Bergen and Fred Allen, she told an interviewer that she once aspired to a career as radio comedian.

She graduated summa cum laude *from Bryn Mawr College, studied under a Fulbright Scholarship at Oxford, and earned her Ph.D. in history from Harvard. A scholar of Renaissance and Reformation history, she holds honorary degrees from forty-two colleges and universities and is a member of the Pulitzer Prize board.*

She currently oversees a university of nearly ten thousand

students and a budget of more than $290 million. "The university's
characteristic state," she told the university senate last winter, "may
be summarized by the words of the lady who said, 'I have enough
money to last me the rest of my life, unless I buy something.' "

Chicago

Is the United States a melting pot or a salad bowl?

That question, says Hanna Gray, is a priority item on the nation's agenda for the 21st century.

If it's a melting pot—as was widely assumed when, at age three, the future president of the University of Chicago emigrated with her parents from Nazi Germany—then it can weather the major population changes she sees ahead. Despite profound shifts in the ratios of whites, blacks, Hispanics, and Asians, she says, the result will be a blending of different elements—an "assimilation of and contribution to something that is distinctively American."

But what if America instead becomes a salad bowl, in which dozens of ethnic ingredients remain separate and un-blended? Instead of "a nation made up of many nationalities," she says, the result would be a collection of individual groups with little to hold them together.

Of one thing she is sure: There will be "a massive change" in the racial and ethnic mix of the nation. What concerns her is "whether this country is really prepared to confront both that change and its implications."

What has bound the nation together in the past, Gray says, is the "expectation that there is a common set of norms, however remote, however difficult to interpret, that frames our society." Those norms include "a commitment to a system of law and constitutional government that people feel really speaks to all of them in a fundamentally similar way."

But "if people don't have that confidence in the systems

of law and governance because they don't experience its benefits," the common bond could disappear.

"I think that by the middle of the next century we most surely need to have moved much further on our current agenda [of race- and population-related issues]."

How can the nation move forward on these issues? Her answer—not surprising from a scholar who entered college at age fifteen and has been in the academic world ever since—is through education, especially at the university level.

What kind of higher education will the 21st century require? Even now, she says, there is "a rather useful debate going on" over that question. On one hand are those who see the university as a source for technical and professional training. On the other are those who, like Gray, want to place more emphasis on the traditional liberal arts programs.

"It's just astonishing, you know, the number of students in many of our very large universities across the country who major in business as undergraduates. Basic science and the basic humanities and social sciences have lost out in many of those institutions."

But she already detects a concern among business leaders and professionals about the loss of those basics—and for "the value system within which all this technological expertise is located."

Her recipe for 21st-century education, in fact, leans heavily on developing that "value system."

In her view, universities need to "inculcate the virtues of critical judgment and of understanding the complexities of things—seeing different sides of questions, and above all understanding how things relate to one another."

What matters to Gray is not so much the information taught as the wisdom that grows out of it. "The explosion of knowledge," she observes, "has surely and forever altered what might be thought of as the terrain of knowledge that you can say with certainty everybody might share together."

So "what we've got to give undergraduates," she explains, "is a central appreciation for the main activities of the human mind and of human culture over time, as well as a central appreciation for the main modes of intellectual activity that operate at the present time." High on her list of goals, too, is to provide students with "a central capacity to sort out the information by which they're going to be overwhelmed."

But hand in hand with these goals comes an ethical outlook that, for Gray, has two facets. The first, which she describes as "the principal ethics that a university should care for and teach," is what she calls "intellectual integrity."

"Intellectual integrity does not tell you what system you should follow. It doesn't tell you which of several values needs to be yours. But it does say that there are wrong answers and that there are cheap answers."

The importance of turning away from "cheap answers" was a point emphasized by her father, the noted European historian Hajo Holborn. She says he felt that "the most terrible thing about the Nazis and what they did to German culture was that they sold people cheap and simple versions of life and history."

"Intellectual integrity teaches you that there are wrong answers," she says simply, adding that "there is an important relationship between personal and intellectual integrity."

As the second facet of the ethical outlook, Gray stresses the need for a proper understanding of what she calls "the use of evidence." Some evidence has "a kind of moral claim, not just a sort of scientific claim, but a moral claim to your attention." Students need to be taught that "you cannot evade evidence that may go in a direction different from your bias or ideology."

The universities of the future, then, will be hard pressed

to maintain the balance between training and education, technology and the humanities, and information and wisdom. What kind of system will best serve the 21st century's needs?

If one word can summarize Gray's convictions on this point, it is *pluralism*—which for her means a thriving mix of private and public institutions. Leaning forward in the chair behind her presidential desk, her features animated by the discussion, she notes with a smile that "this is a subject that I'm passionate about."

It is a passion driven by long years of experience in private education, much of it spent worrying about the steeply rising costs of learning and the implied threat from taxpayer-supported institutions with lower tuition.

"We've seen a shift from private universities to public universities, and we see fewer private universities." That's not necessarily bad, she says, except that it suggests that the nation lacks "a national sense of purpose and value about a pluralistic university system."

"Why is it, then, that all universities shouldn't be public?" she asks. Answering her own question, she notes that in other countries "systems of higher education that are monolithic and that are state-run ultimately become politicized—ultimately become instruments rather than critics of and contributors to the society."

The result is that they "ultimately can descend to mediocrity, ultimately lack the competitive edge that makes it possible for different ways, different approaches, creative ideas, the taking of risks, to happen."

Given the economic pressures on education, she wonders whether the current pluralism in American education—which she considers to be "the best system of higher education in the world"—can be maintained in the 21st century.

Some other educators, sharing her concern, have called

for stronger national policies toward education. On that point, Gray has mixed feelings. Americans have "always been very suspicious of national cultural ministries and national educational ministries." On the other hand, the public has a "clear recognition of the disparities that exist and of the inequalities of opportunity" that characterize the present situation.

She takes a dim view, she says, of some of the "pronouncements" of Education Secretary William J. Bennett—which, despite his avowed support for pluralism, tend to produce "a strange and paradoxical centralization of values."

But she feels strongly about what she calls "a national policy of access to higher education."

That means, she says, "a commitment to making it possible for people, regardless of their backgrounds, means, genders, race, to aspire to the level of education that they're suited for," and a commitment to providing the necessary loans and grants for that access.

She also sees the need for broader awareness of "the significance of research and what it means to a society," as well as "a national recognition that the future is ultimately grounded in the capacity to confront change and to adapt."

So far, Gray has been speaking about the national agenda. What about the world agenda?

"It seems to me that there are really three major questions before the world," she says, ticking them off without further explanation. The first is "the nuclear question and the question as to how containable the threat of nuclear devastation is."

The second concerns "the relationship between the less developed countries and the developed world," with the issue centering on "whether it is possible to sustain both a world economy and the hopes for democratic and humanitarian governments . . . in the less-developed countries."

Her third point takes the form of a question. Is it necessary, she asks, for the "more developed countries, which at the same time are full of injustice—for example, South Africa—to go through the destructive, violent kind of change that one sees almost inevitably as coming?" Or can they evolve in "more peaceful ways"?

Gray, a member of the Chicago Council on Foreign Relations and the Council on Foreign Relations of New York, is concerned that, in global matters, the U.S. is playing a shrunken role.

Compared with the post–World War II period, "I think we have a less international view." As the nation becomes "less prosperous," it also becomes "more insular." Rather than "seeing itself more as part of the world, the U.S. tends to withdraw and to become more inward, and that's a weakening in and of itself."

What she sees as an ebbing of national prosperity brings her, finally, to two other points on the U.S. agenda involving what she calls a "shift in expectations about the future."

The first has to do with economics on a personal level. "The assumption of continuing growth, the assumption of the opportunities for social mobility, are surely being somewhat questioned. And it seems to me that the United States is again on the verge of worrying whether it really is the world power—and also worrying whether [its former prosperity] will ever come back.

"That issue about exaggerated expectations—and an extreme reaction if they're not met—is one that I think is not as yet well dealt with in our society." She sees a need for coming generations to temper their economic expectations and "become realistic."

The second shift in expectations concerns the women's movement. "Sometimes, the rhetoric of the women's movement suggests that absolutely everything needs to be possible." It leads women, she says, to ask why "this one major biological difference should stand in the way" and to assume that "society is meant to be able to deal with it.

"Well, there are issues that society can mitigate, issues that it can build institutions around and help," she says. "But in the end it cannot make for people some of the choices that are theirs to make."

The "choices" are difficult ones—concerning not only whether to have children but what kinds of careers to pursue. "I worry that some of the younger women, who have opportunities undreamt of at an earlier time, are going to have extreme reactions when they discover that it's really a little more difficult."

The result will be an upsurge in the "belief that society ought to create the institutions that will make life less painful for all of us."

But the kinds of issues facing women in the 21st century, she says, "cannot be entirely solved for them by society."

Amitai Etzioni

Seeking the Center

Ask American sociologist Amitai Etzioni what sort of thinker he admires, and he points to "the very few people who take an intermediary position."

"That's what I find so interesting. In life, everything is obviously somewhere in between."

The German-born author has, however, had his share of extremes. After fleeing with his parents to Palestine in 1936 to escape Nazi anti-Semitism, he joined the underground troops in the struggle for Israeli independence from the British. He later fought Arab troops during Israel's War of Independence.

After earning bachelor's and master's degrees at Hebrew University, he immigrated to the United States in 1957, entering the University of California at Berkeley and emerging in only eighteen months with a Ph.D. in sociology.

In 1980, after twenty years on the faculty at Columbia University, he became university professor at George Washington University, where he heads the Center for Policy Research. He is currently a visiting professor at the Harvard Business School.

Author of more than a dozen books—including An Immodest Agenda *(1982) and* Capital Corruption *(1984)—he is a frequent contributor of op-ed articles to newspapers and testifier at congressional hearings, and has served as a White House adviser.*

*Etzioni has been dubbed "the everything expert." But his
wide-ranging interests—spanning subjects as diverse as organiza-
tional theory, nuclear disarmament, genetic technology, and the rein-
dustrialization of America—have won him respect for his ability to
put individual issues into broad perspective.*

Aspen, Colorado

Over a late-afternoon iced tea in a street-front café here,
Amitai Etzioni spins out an anecdote that captures, for him,
the central challenge facing America in the future.

"There was a building inspector in San Francisco who
used a helicopter to increase his efficiency in doing his job,"
he says, recalling a news clip he had seen. "His job was to see
that people were not augmenting buildings without prior
approval of the city. By flying over the buildings he could do
ten buildings or a hundred buildings instead of walking up
the stairs one at a time."

The homeowners, recalls Etzioni, were outraged.
The reason? They said it was "unfair to use a helicopter
against—*against!*—the citizens. And the courts, and public
opinion, lined up behind that outcry, and they had his
helicopter grounded."

"I've collected many other examples," he says with a
smile, "which all have the same flavor."

The "flavor" Etzioni is talking about has to do with
the excesses of a "me-istic" society—a society so caught up
in its own individuality that it has neglected the sense of
community.

Asked to address himself to the major issue facing the
world in the 21st century, Etzioni goes directly to "what
I call the I-and-we issue."

Unlike many contemporary thinkers who take hard
looks at the future, Etzioni is encouraged by what he sees.

"We've been for twenty years very me-istic, very, very strong on the individual, very neglectful of the we-ness. And we're having a comeback not of collectivism but of a better balance between the I and the we. And I'm celebrating it."

A well-functioning society, says Etzioni, has a need for both positions. "You don't want either polar position. You want what is called an I-and-we strain. You want a continuous, unending conflict where on the one hand the community keeps saying, 'There's too much individualism: Listen to me, don't booze, don't smoke, drugs are bad,' and on the other hand people saying, 'No, I have a need,' and feeling inside themselves a tug-of-war."

That kind of tug-of-war has been going on in America since "the founding days," he says, adding that "we have it today, and we're going to have it in the 21st century."

What, then, are the major issues that the next century must address? Etzioni identifies several:

Changes in governmental institutions Topping Etzioni's list is what he sees as some much-needed structural change in Congress, especially concerning the use of PAC (political-action committee) money. His solution: public funding of congressional campaigns (following the British model), and a pay increase coupled with a prohibition on outside income. With such measures, he asserts, "you would clean up politics there and then."

Beyond that, however, Etzioni sees a need for "a major social movement" dedicated to tackling structural reforms in the legal, social, and political arenas. "We need a movement in support of the rules of the game, without any leftist tinges."

Without a truly middle-of-the-road movement for reform, he notes, "you won't have the public underpinning that you need for institutional change."

Demographic shifts   "By the year 2000," he says, "*old* will be considered eighty-five years or older, not sixty-five or older." Retirement at sixty-five, he says, is "a completely obsolescent concept." He foresees a continued downward adjustment in social security benefits as this recognition takes hold.

Energy supplies   "There's a limit to the amount of oil," says Etzioni simply. It's true that "we found a lot more than expected, and the market is doing its wonderful thing. In the end, though, we're burning it up like mad, and nobody's adding a single barrel to the pool down there. So one of these days we'll have to deal with that issue again."

Every time he sees another highway under construction, "I ask myself, 'Has anybody sat down to ask whether in forty or fifty years we are really going to be still swimming in oil?' "

Debt   Here Etzioni offers a mini-history lesson. "From 1820 to 1920 we plowed a lot back into the economy." But after the Depression and World War II, "we had one generation that basically spent more than we produced—running down what three generations saved. So then we went to everybody else in the world, especially the Japanese, and they lent us several hundred billions so we could go on with this Coke commercial, with this party, with this hedonism, without tightening our belt. We're very close to the end of it, because people just won't lend us that much more.

"We've run down our inheritance. We've borrowed from everybody all we can borrow. Who's going to give us the next 200 billion?"

Leadership   Etzioni is particularly interested in the question of leadership or, more precisely, the lack of it.

"The concept of leadership," he explains, "is 50 percent followership.

"Most people think about leadership as this: You come up with a new idea that nobody has heard of, and you're going to implement it," he says. "President Reagan tried that twice: He tried it on the church-state issue, and he tried it on social security."

The result, says Etzioni, was that the president "did not lead, because there was no followership.

"The reason we don't have great leaders at the moment is that the followership is not ready."

Why not? Because "followership" grows out of a sense of commitment to the community—just the kind of "we-ism" that has been missing in recent decades.

Issue by issue, Etzioni returns to his I-we distinction to explain several of the major concerns facing the nation as the 21st century approaches.

"People are all gung ho on defense, but when it comes to the notion of serving their country, there's a very thin support. There is no wide sense that the average middle-class American, especially white, especially male, has to serve his or her country."

On the issue of taxes there is "a great cynicism, not a widespread feeling that the system is fair." When the Internal Revenue Service comes up for discussion in Congress, he says, there are always those who argue that the laws do not provide "a fair match between Internal Revenue and the citizens who violate the tax law—as if this is some kind of a running match."

As for federal programs, Etzioni refers to a conference of manufacturers he recently addressed.

He recalls that the other speakers, each from a different industry, "attacked the government for its large deficits and for all the impositions it puts on the country and the way it intervenes in the economy." But "somewhere down in the speech," he noticed, each speaker "came in and argued,

'Well, my energy industry cannot develop unless the government gives us special credits,' or, 'We exporters need a federal export-import bank.'

"None of them found any conflict. They didn't even realize what they were doing—repeating all the laissez-faire clichés, and then saying, 'Give-me.' "

Etzioni is not plumping for increased state control as a way to counter excessive individualism. But neither is he pleased with the tendency toward libertarian, laissez-faire attitudes in recent decades.

His goal: to strike a moderate position, restoring the balance where the competing strains of individualism and community life hold each other in check.

How will that help shape the future? Etzioni uses the I-we concept to make sense of both personal and political issues.

In the former area, he cites the increased interest in the family and the return to religion as the most important indicators. He sees a widespread shift away from the sexual revolution of the Me Generation as increasing numbers of people are discovering that merely "biological relationships are not very satisfying" and are seeking instead "the beauty of mutuality, of the lasting relationship."

He also sees hopeful signs of "we-ness" in the career choices young people are making. "In the me-istic era the way to build your career was to worry about yourself and nothing else. You wouldn't listen to someone talk about social needs, collective needs, the future of the nation.

"That's changing now. Today there is increasing interest among youngsters, not in [such organizations as] the Peace Corps, but in finding careers in which somehow you can combine 'making it' with something meaningful."

And what about the political arena? Here, Etzioni is less sanguine.

In politics, he notes, "we still have rampant me-ism, only on the group level. Rather than each individual coming and saying, 'Give me,' each special-interest group comes and says 'Give me'—and there's no willingness to balance.

"It's not a question of whether we all stop worrying about our special interests and worry only about the nation," he says, noting that such a shift would not only be undesirable but "inconceivable."

But the "opposite situation," where no one is concerned about the nation, is equally undesirable. Yet that situation is what "we're very close to" now.

The "me-istic" tendency that became so noticeable in the 1960s and '70s did not appear out of nowhere. To Etzioni, its roots are understandable—and must be grasped if present social trends are to be comprehended.

On one side he sees the pressures toward "we-ness." Reflecting on the historical evolution of societies, he notes that "a community tries to suck in and absorb the individual, whether it's the church or the monarchy or the totalitarian state, and not leave room for individualism."

On the other side, however, arises what he calls "anti-we-ness," which he defines as a "major strain" in American society.

"The theme of many of our western movies is that authority is crooked. So you give the citizen the same power, the same gun, or whatever, as the authority, because he basically suspects the authority, the we-ness, the community."

While such deep-dyed individuality is an essential part of the American character, he says that the nation has tilted dangerously far from what he calls a "moral commitment" to the community at large.

At bottom, Etzioni sees the general need for a renewal of this commitment.

"In the end, you cannot police people." Instead, "you have to make certain things unthinkable."

What does he mean by *unthinkable?*

Suppose, he says, that you're a middle-class citizen short of money. "None of us, I think, will consider sending our children to panhandle to raise the money—you just don't think about it. You don't sit down and say, 'Now, should I?' "

"Now, we need more things to go into that box," he says, like "selling highly carcinogenic agents, or dumping toxic things into the water mains."

He already sees the "beginning of a 'we-ness' trend" in these directions.

"The boot is set," he says. "All we need is the sock."

A Search for Balance

III

What's right? Where do you stop? How far do you go in fulfilling goals that increase cost and that offset your ability to become competitive and provide more jobs? How do you balance these things? There's no morally absolute right and wrong about these things.

—Marina Whitman

Marina Whitman

Douglas Fraser

Robert S. McNamara

Marina Whitman

Ringside at the Economy

For Amitai Etzioni, everything in life is "somewhere in between." What matters to him is the sense of mutuality that seeks out the center, melds conflicting views into workable compromise, and finds the "we-ness" that allows democracy to function.

That sense of mutuality—made tangible by the day-to-day demands of the workplace—characterizes the careers of the three individuals in this section: Marina Whitman, Douglas Fraser, and Robert McNamara. All of them, one way or another, have shaped their views of the world on the workbench of economics. All have been deeply involved with automaking—which, as America's premier heavy industry, remains the crucible where the challenges of international competition, labor relations, and the balance of public-sector regulation and private-sector enterprise are blended and tested. Perhaps most importantly, all have had to operate squarely in the public limelight, learning to transmute the theoretical vision of the philosopher and the historian into the long-wearing metal of practical affairs. And if the success of their individual careers indicates that the metal is sound, the clarity of their ideas, in the interviews that follow, suggests that the vision has remained gloriously intact.

In 1979, shortly before she joined General Motors as a vice-president and chief economist, recalls Marina Whitman, "my husband ran out of gas looking for gas." The shock of the Arab oil

---

embargo was being felt not only at the gas pump but throughout the American economy—especially among the auto-makers, who were scrambling to design down-sized, fuel-efficient cars. "I should have realized that life would never be the same. What I walked into was probably the biggest economic or industrial revolution—and in some ways the biggest social phenomenon—of the late 20th century."

Her career as an economist had prepared her for the task of helping to revitalize the nation's largest manufacturer. Whitman, the daughter of mathematician John von Neumann, a father of the modern computer, graduated from Radcliffe in 1956 at the top of her class. After earning a Ph.D. in economics from Columbia University, she taught economics from 1962 to 1979 at the University of Pittsburgh, where her husband teaches English.

Appointed by President Nixon as one of three members of his Council of Economic Advisers, she has also been associated with the Trilateral Commission, the Council on Foreign Relations, the American Enterprise Institute, the Brookings Institution, and many other academic, government, and advisory organizations. The author of a number of books and articles on international economic theory, she has conducted a weekly television program on economics that was carried on 180 public broadcasting stations.

In 1985 Whitman was promoted to vice-president in charge of GM's public-affairs staff group—where, as an economist friend recently wrote her, she has "a ringside seat" for watching the international economy.

Detroit

Marina Whitman launches her discussion of the 21st century with the inbred caution of an economist making a forecast. "The whole premise is impossible," she says with a smile, over a tuna sandwich in her book-filled fourteenth-floor office in the stately old General Motors Building. "If you really knew what kind of knowledge or thoughts you were going to have in the future, you'd have them now."

All she can do, she says, is to "identify contemporary trends and developments that seem to be threads in the fabric of the future."

For her, that translates into a single, overriding issue governing all the items on the next century's agenda. She calls it "a search for balance."

In her view, the problems facing humanity have less to do with black-and-white choices than with the need for subtle weighing of alternatives. "You give up resources of some things to get others," she says. "Not that there are never synergies: There are. But there are also constant trade-offs."

Whitman notes what she calls "the catastrophic scenarios" of a nuclear holocaust or a 14th-century kind of plague induced by AIDS (acquired immune deficiency syndrome). "One has to dismiss those scenarios," she says, "not because they're impossible but simply because you can't say anything sensible about them, really."

Her concern, in fact, is less with such extremes than with the middle ground of everyday experience. "It seems to me that at least going into the 21st century—which is, after all, only a little more than a decade away—we will have a kind of search for balance in a number of areas."

One such area: the balancing between national identities and a worldwide market.

One "obvious" trend is "a very rapid global integration of markets—markets for goods, markets for services, markets for technology, markets for ideas.

"At the same time, as far as goods are concerned," she adds, there has been "a certain erosion of national identity."

As evidence, she cites the fact that "it's getting harder and harder to tell what's an American car or a Japanese radio. It may be made by Motorola, but part of it was put together in Singapore and another part in Mexico, and it was finally assembled in the United States."

Nevertheless, "there is still a very strong sense in people of nationalism, of a need for community. Nobody can quite deal with the global village as a community."

The result is that "there's a kind of a tension. . . . You have this global integration of everything, and you have at the same time a strong sense of nationalism in the populations of most, if not all countries."

"I am an internationalist by training and by emotions," she says, "and I have strong feelings about the need for international cooperation in the economic sphere. When I was very young I had the sort of internationalist visions that were popular at the time—that you could kind of abolish national boundaries."

Now, she says, "I don't think that's such a terrific idea, because I think people do need some kind of framework and community." For that reason, she says, "the nation-state has become a kind of logical focus."

On the one hand, the thrust toward globalization has produced, in her view, solid benefits. "There's no question that a lot of the rapid growth of world output and living standards in the postwar period was underlined by a progressive freeing up of markets and increases in international trade."

But because of the countercurrent of nationalism, she says, "there are always pressures to put up barriers to that global integration—whether they are trade barriers, or discrimination against foreign investors, or very restrictive immigration laws.

"I think one of the things we're going to go into the 21st century with, somewhat unresolved, is this question of how you reconcile these in the optimal way." The goal, Whitman adds, will be to "reap all the benefits of global integration of markets—in terms of efficiency and consumer choice and the increasing incorporation of larger and larger parts of the world into this international interaction—and at the same time not interfere too much with people's sense of national identity."

Closely related to that issue, and high on the agenda of items for the next century to deal with, is a second point: the growth of global competition. "You have lots of new players in the game, and the cast of characters changes very fast.

"You have countries not only like Japan—which went from being one of the lowest per-capita income countries after World War II to one of the highest in the world—but like Taiwan, South Korea, and Brazil, and so forth, which are fast joining this crowd. And with that come very rapid shifts in patterns of production and employment—because of the diffusion of technology and because of rapid changes in comparative advantage and production patterns and trade patterns.

"The phenomena are nothing new, but the speed with which they're occurring is.

"All of that tends to increase uncertainty, and people don't like uncertainty . . . which is caused by change. On the other hand, of course, if you put a stop to change you would have a pretty disastrous world."

The answer, for her, lies once again in a delicate balance. "One is constantly searching—and I think will still be searching as we move into the next century—for ways of cushioning adjustment, of minimizing the pain of economic dislocation, which don't, at the same time, unduly hold up the process of change and progress. And that's hard," she concludes.

A third item on Whitman's agenda has to do with the effects of what she calls "privatization," "denationalization," or "deregulation."

On the one hand, there is "a tendency for greater reliance on the marketplace." On the other, "we are tending, in quite a different sense, to 'socialize' those very same institutions" that have been deregulated.

"I'm not talking now about 'socialism' with the capital S but 'socialize' with the small s." Her point is that since World War II "society has been holding businesses responsible for the fulfillment of a wide variety of social goals."

"Some of that comes through the [governmental] regulatory process," she explains, by which corporations have increasingly been held responsible "for the quality of the environment, for safety, for fuel efficiency, for employment, for job security, for fairness, for democratization of the decision-making process as far as stockholders are concerned."

Here she takes issue, mildly, with noted free-market economist Milton Friedman—who, she recalls, "once said that the sole social purpose of a corporation is to make a profit."

"There's a certain sense in which that's true," she says, noting that for a company, "the profit is the ante. If you don't make profits you can't stay in the game and you can't do anything else useful. But it's also clear that society does not regard that as the only goal. There is a kind of implicit social compact under which corporations, businesses, exist, in which they are expected to do a good deal more than that and are expected to fulfill a great many goals."

Some of those goals are "inherently and internally in conflict"—such as the pressure to build safer cars that are also smaller and more fuel-efficient. The conflict "may be as simple as the laws of physics that tell you that when you downsize a car, all other things being equal, it's not going to be as safe."

As the next century approaches, she foresees a "reduced pace" of "social regulation" promulgated by government. "I think we've had a good deal of experience with government regulation"—enough to prove that it can "turn out to be a rather costly and not always very effective way" to achieve society's goals. But that doesn't mean that "society has any lower expectations of these entities called businesses or corporations."

The goal must be, again, a careful balance. "On the one hand, it's almost impossible to multiply these [social] demands without increasing cost. But to the extent which you raise production costs, you will tend to reduce the competitiveness—and thereby reduce the corporation's ability to fulfill another social goal, which has to do with providing stable and well-paid jobs.

"If you ask me, as the person in charge of public affairs at General Motors, who has come out of an economics background, what are the two big challenges confronting this corporation—and to some extent any corporation—it's the need to become and remain globally competitive, which is an absolute imperative, and to meet this plethora of social goals that are a part of this implicit compact with society."

Turning to still another area where, in the future, there will be "tension and the need for balance," Whitman points to what she calls "a tremendous decline in the sources of authority."

"Whether it's in terms of the family, or of the church, or of the school, or of the state or the government, clearly the sense of authority possessed by any such group has very substantially eroded."

"I do think that it is important that we find ways of reestablishing some center of moral authority," she says. And, while she insists that "I'm not going to sit here and say which ones they should be," she admits that "I've got a personal preference."

"I think the family is a pretty good institution. I think it's a good deal more flexible institution than many of its strongest supporters want to admit."

Does today's shifting of ethics have economic consequences? Here she points to the workplace. "When people teach courses in business ethics," she says, "they tend to talk about the idea that you shouldn't steal." That, she says, "goes without saying. The really interesting question of business ethics is how do you reconcile conflicting goals?"

She poses the question of how to build an automobile that is 100 percent safe. Theoretically, she says, it could perhaps be done. But you would end up "with something of infinite cost and zero value."

"What's right?" she asks. "Where do you stop? How far do you go in fulfilling goals that increase cost and that offset your ability to become competitive and provide more jobs? How do you balance these things? There's no morally absolute right and wrong about these things."

She sees a willingness to consider these things—and a greater interest in authority—in the rising generation. "The generation that's coming up now seems to be combining a kind of conservatism—and certainly a good deal of commitment to the work ethic, which some people say comes out of the '50s—with a kind of sense of the need for individual self-fulfillment that comes out of the '60s and '70s."

"We may not be totally pleased" with their attitudes, she says, citing the level of "concern about the materialism of the younger generation." But, she adds, "I think they're groping for some kind of synthesis."

The result, she says, will be yet another "tension" that society will carry into the 21st century. One place it will show up is in "what you might call workplace relations."

"*Labor relations*," she points out, "is almost an obsolete term." Instead, both labor and management are sensing "a very strong need to move from an adversarial to a cooperative model—whether it's driven by the demands of international competition, by the lessons we learn from the Japanese, or by the needs of an increasingly more educated and more self-conscious work force."

"The fact is," she says with a smile, "that people exist from the shoulders up as well as the shoulders down. And the guy who does the job may be indeed the greatest living expert on what the problems are and how it could be done better."

Focusing on those kinds of "workplace relations," she says, is "critically important" for the future—not only at General Motors but across American industry. But even that requires a delicate balance—since any corporation has to remain "rapidly responsive to changes in consumers' taste or to changes in the external environment."

"That requires the maintenance of a decision-making capacity.

"You can't democratize things in such a way that you paralyze them. And that ties into the point before: You have to legitimize authority, but you have to legitimize it in nonauthoritarian ways where people are participants in it."

Douglas Fraser

Paying the Piper

"I was never sorry I went through the Depression," says Douglas Fraser, who retired in 1983 as president of the 1.1 million-member United Automobile Workers (UAW). "It made such a lasting impression on me that I never forgot where I came from."

Born in a working-class section of Glasgow, Fraser was six when he moved with his family to Detroit, where his father, a labor union activist, worked as an electrician in a Studebaker plant. Fraser dropped out of high school and went to work as a metal finisher in Chrysler Corporation's DeSoto plant.

He became president of his UAW local in 1943, served in World War II, and joined the UAW administrative staff under Walter Reuther in 1953. Succeeding Leonard Woodcock in a six-year term as UAW president in 1977, Fraser negotiated the first wage and benefit concessions in the history of the union in the face of an industrywide sales slump.

As a director of Chrysler, he was the first prominent labor leader to sit on an American corporate board. Recently, he has been sharing his knowledge and experience at various universities, including Harvard and Wayne State University, where he teaches courses in labor studies.

"We're not an organization that's just interested in membership and dues and negotiating wage increases and rich fringe

benefits," says Fraser, referring to the UAW. "We're about the community. We're an instrument for social change. The important thing is equipping your members or your former members to live fulfilling lives."

Detroit

What will the 21st century look like to the working man and woman?

After decades of watching the world from a blue-collar perspective, Douglas Fraser puts "a top priority" on international relations and global peace. Those issues, he says, will be "absolutely critical" to the 21st century—because "the consequences of not doing something" could be "horrible . . . beyond imagination."

High on his agenda, too, is the need for reform in the American political system and in the way nations manage debt.

But in an hour-long conversation at the Detroit Metro airport during a break in his busy traveling schedule, Fraser focused primarily on issues that arise on the shop floor. There, in particular, he sees some significant adjustments for the 21st century.

He predicts a future of increased career changing, shortened work hours, and lengthened retirement years. Despite the availability of home computers, he thinks employees will still want to go to work in central locations—largely for the sake of the camaraderie. They may even get there in electric cars.

But above all, he sees steady technological advances in such areas as computer electronics and robotics—advances that will alter both work itself and the social and political structure of the work force.

For Fraser, that's just as it should be. He is concerned

about the so-called technological unemployment that occurs when machines replace workers. But he remains convinced that new technologies bring tremendous benefits—if the world deals properly with their effects on humanity.

"It's not economically sound to resist or even slow down the introduction of new technology," he says, building his argument with full awareness of the controversy that sometimes bubbles up at the factory gates when workers feel threatened by robots.

"New technology does not necessarily mean unemployment or loss of jobs," he insists. "If you have the introduction of new technology and an expansion in the economy at the same time, you won't have any unemployment."

To dramatize his point, he cites figures from a business he knows inside out: the American automotive industry.

In the twenty years following 1957, he says, the industry experienced "the introduction of automation in the stamping plants and the machining plants and the foundries." But because the domestic production of cars and trucks grew rapidly—from 7.5 million units in 1957 to 12.5 million in 1977—the labor force actually expanded by 13 percent in that period.

For Fraser, it's a comforting example, proving that jobs can grow despite automation. Which, he says, is a good thing, because "even if you're so inclined," you can't stop the influx of new technology.

Why not? Drawing again from the auto industry, he gives two reasons. The first has to do with global competition: "Japan is not going to stop and Germany is not going to stop" introducing new technology.

The second has to do with "something that is not commonly recognized in many cases," which is that "new technology means improved quality, because you eliminate the human error. And obviously we're in a quality contest . . .

with the Japanese and other [carmakers] throughout the world."

As this new technology continues to shape the next century's assembly lines, however, it will also bring significant changes to the lives of the workers.

"We're going to go to shorter work time, just as sure as we sit here."

Will a shortening of the work hours produce a four-day work week in the early years of the 21st century?

"No, I don't think it will happen that quickly," he responds, although he notes that "Germany is now down to thirty-eight hours [in a work week]." For economic reasons, he says, the change will be gradual, because "if you go from five-day to four-day weeks, you're increasing the costs by more than 20 percent.

"You just can't absorb that kind of economic shock in one fell swoop."

Much more immediate, according to Fraser, will be changes in the relation of work years to retirement years. He looks to the complete elimination of a mandatory retirement age, producing a workplace in which "there will be absolutely no [upper] age restraints at all."

In fact, however, he sees little effect from that change—largely because he expects increasing numbers of employees to retire well before age sixty-five. Again, he draws his example from the carmakers, where workers can retire after thirty years.

"Theoretically," he says, referring to employees who go to work at age eighteen, "retirement age can be forty-eight." For years, he notes, the union resisted that idea, on the grounds that forty-eight was "almost the prime of life." Gradually, however, that resistance has diminished. "Who am I to say that forty-eight is not the right age for a person's worth after thirty years in the shop," he says, adding, "thirty years in the shop, assembling cars, is not a very thrilling life."

Part of the reason it's not very thrilling, he concedes, is because there are "a lot of lousy jobs" in the auto industry—wet sanding, torch soldering, and so forth. Automation, he says, can eliminate some of those jobs—such as soldering, which because of the danger of lead poisoning is no longer a central part of American carmaking. Fraser also sees a shift away from the mind-dulling routines of assembly-line work and toward a process of manufacturing in "modules"—where teams of workers, each doing a sequence of different jobs, build a substantial part of each car.

As work time shrinks, Fraser expects a corresponding increase in leisure time—and an increase in the level of debate about what to do with it. He sees nothing surprising in these developments. "That's history: Work a twelve-hour day, and then a ten-hour day, and then finally an eight-hour day."

Nor is there anything surprising to him in the debate about the value of leisure time. For centuries, he notes, industrialists have warned that "a shorter work time would really be dangerous, because the workers would have too much idle time on their hands, and idleness results in mischief."

Today, however, Fraser sees not mischief but a steady return to education, among both the retired and those still working.

"I don't know how many of our retirees are going to community colleges, picking up new skills. I've got a couple in my class," he says, referring to the course he teaches at Wayne State University. "It's wonderful." He sees a need in the future to make education more available to workers and retirees.

All of which assumes, of course, that America's future will continue to be full of manufacturing jobs. Fraser concedes that there will be "an erosion of jobs in heavy industry." That has already happened. Yet he is encouraged by "the rate at which this country has generated jobs," describing it as "absolutely incredible" compared with other countries.

The problem lies in the nature of the jobs created. The real growth in the United States, Fraser notes, has come in service-sector jobs—which typically pay less, sometimes much less, than manufacturing jobs. He cites recent studies done in Youngstown, Ohio, where steelworkers laid off when they were earning $12 an hour could find only service-sector jobs—in fast-food restaurants, for example—at $5 an hour.

"So you dramatically decrease your purchasing power, and therefore the standard of living." If that happens to too many Americans, he says, the result will be felt throughout the economy. "Who's going to buy the services if all of these great middle-class jobs disappear?"

One answer, of course, is that the buyers will be the workers in the overseas nations that pick up the heavy-industry jobs America loses. In particular, Fraser cites South Korea, Taiwan, Malaysia, Brazil, and especially China as the newly emerging manufacturing powers of the 21st century. He says those countries will become increasingly important markets for American goods and services—as long as Americans continue to exhibit their "talent and genius" for developing new products and new markets.

What about Japan? Will its industrial might compel the 21st-century American work force to conform to Japanese patterns of single-mindedness and determined obedience?

No, says Fraser, who has toured factories in Japan. "We're too individualistic." Instead, he says, "I would predict that the Japanese will conform to the Western culture." Why? Because "there's something insidious—thank goodness—about freedom and liberty and democracy."

And that brings Fraser to some of his deepest concerns about the 21st century: the inability of the American political process to provide sound government.

"If our Founding Fathers looked at us now . . . and saw our inability to manage the debt," he says, they might think that "we should have gone to the parliamentary system. Maybe we imposed so many checks and balances in the system that we immobilized ourselves."

Fraser is particularly concerned about the level of debt—personal, national, and international. "I've been talking about it for years," he says, "but I don't blame people for not listening, because we were predicting a catastrophic event—by now, by 1986."

That collapse, he notes, has not come. "But as sure as night follows day, we've got to pay the piper. It's just a question of *when* we pay the piper. And the longer we wait, the more difficult it's going to be."

One way he can see the debt being better managed is by cuts in defense spending. "I'm not a unilateral disarmament person," says Fraser, who served on President Carter's General Advisory Committee on Arms Control and Disarmament. "I believe we live in a dangerous and treacherous world and we have to be strong."

He is convinced, however, that such strength can be maintained with lower levels of defense spending.

But the heart of the problem, for Fraser, lies in what he calls "a lack of will and political courage" in Congress and at the White House. Instead of facing up to tough issues, he says, elected officials "run for cover."

"I don't think my memory's faulty," he adds. "I just think they had more courage in the past."

Fraser charges the problem to a weakening of the political parties, which is "bad for democracy."

"It's hard to get a cohesive program or policy unless

you have a strong party. I don't know quite what we do about it. Maybe repeal all the PACs [political action committees] and . . . have public finance through the political parties—something to give the parties strength.

"Otherwise, you're just going to have 435 individuals in the House and 100 in the Senate—no cohesion, no policy, no program."

"I was on a couple of reform commissions," he recalls. "We tried to strengthen the parties. But it's television that's doing us in." Through TV "you can personalize politics. So now candidates are not dependent upon political parties. They ignore their political parties. They don't have to pay any attention to the platform adopted by the convention, which should be the manifesto."

What can be done about TV's influence on campaigns? "I'd abolish thirty-second [political] commercials. I would make the candidates come on themselves," as in Britain, where, he explains, "everybody gets equal time on television" without paying for it.

Robert S. McNamara

Traditional Values, High-Leverage Issues

"I'm here to originate, to stimulate new ideas and programs, and not just to adjudicate arguments," said Robert S. McNamara when, in 1961, he joined the Kennedy administration as secretary of defense. "You've got to do things differently or else you're not improving them."

McNamara's whole career, in fact, bears witness to his desire to "do things differently." A straight-A high-school student in California, he majored in economics and philosophy at the University of California at Berkeley, where he was elected to Phi Beta Kappa after his sophomore year. After studying at the Graduate School of Business Administration at Harvard University, McNamara joined the faculty there in 1940, leaving within several years to join the Eighth Air Force in Britain.

After the war he joined the Ford Motor Company— becoming, in 1960, the first president of that company not from the Ford family. It was, however, a short-lived honor: Within weeks he had left for Washington, where he would remain in the cabinet in both the Kennedy and Johnson administrations.

In 1968 McNamara became president of the World Bank, a position he held for thirteen years. Since 1981 he has served on a number of corporate boards and worked with nonprofit organizations on such issues as nuclear arms, population and development, world hunger, and East-West relations. *He is the author of several books, the most recent being* Blundering into Disaster: Surviving the First Century of the Nuclear Age.

New York

Robert McNamara has had four careers: Harvard professor, Ford Motor Company executive, secretary of defense, and president of the World Bank. But as he bounds up the curving staircase to his room at the River Club in New York City, taking the steps two at a time, you might peg him for a fifth career—as athlete.

Upstairs, as he turns his attention to the agenda for the 21st century, his mind proves equally athletic. He speaks with the rapid-fire vitality of a thinker seized by the subject and impelled by its urgency. The two central issues he singles out for his agenda are not surprising for a man with his background in defense and development issues.

The first is the nuclear threat, the subject of his latest book. "After all," he says, "if we can't survive as a civilized world, then there's no time to work on any other subject."

The other item he describes as "the population problem," which he says has the potential to cause "very, very serious economic, social, political, and perhaps even military problems" for the 21st century.

Ranked below these two "high-leverage" issues are three others:

- East-West political tensions, which he argues are "distorting our allocation of economic resources"
- A loss of some of the traditional moral values of American democracy
- The need for new forms of institutions fitted to a changing world.

On this last point, McNamara does not expect to see the development of a world government. But he notes that "in fifty to one hundred years from now, we [in the United States] will find it's in our interest to transfer from national sovereignty to international institutions certain of the powers that we exercise now as a nation-state.

"The longer we delay in addressing some of these issues—the East-West tensions, the institutional forms appropriate for an increasingly interdependent world, the return to our national traditions—the greater difficulty we're going to face in the 21st century."

Turning to his first agenda item, McNamara discounts the argument that the West's nuclear strategy—which he finds seriously flawed—has preserved peace since World War II. "I think it's extremely dangerous," he asserts, "to carry on our present strategy and our present weapons-development programs, in the direction they're headed, for another forty years."

The danger arises "because of the environment we're in. We are in a world with fifty thousand nuclear warheads—each one, on average, some thirty times the destructive power of that dropped on Hiroshima and Nagasaki.

"War plans covering their use are in existence—and there is, in effect, a mind-set that would assure their use in the event of confrontation between East and West," he explains, condensing arguments he has developed at greater length in his book.

"And yet," he adds, "no plan exists for initiating the use of nuclear weapons without the probable destruction of the civilization of the initiator."

How dangerous is the threat of such conflict?

"I don't believe that any well-informed, cooly rational military or civilian leader on either side, East or West, would initiate the use of nuclear weapons. But it has been my experience—and I think it is a widely shared experience—that military and civilian leaders in times of crisis are neither well informed nor coolly rational.

"And I, for one, am not prepared to accept the risk that these [East-West] political rivalries will not, over a period of decades, upon occasion lead to military confrontation."

What, then, can be done?

"Well, clearly, one should address the basic issue, which is the political rivalry between East and West. We have become almost paranoiac, as a people, with respect to the Soviet Union. We exaggerate their strengths, we underestimate our own, and we keep ourselves in a continual state of anxiety with respect to them."

This anxiety, he continues, "has a lot to do with a movement away from our traditional values."

For two hundred years, he argues, the United States has "supported freedom and liberty and democracy." But over the last forty years American governments have backed Nationalist Chinese leader Chiang Kai-shek, the Shah of Iran, Philippine President Ferdinand Marcos, and Nicaraguan President Anastasio Somoza Debayle.

"Support of those regimes is not consistent with the social, political, moral values I wish to pass on to my children."

The problem, he says, has arisen because the citizenry has accepted "actions inconsistent with our national heritage and national traditions, in order to strengthen our position vis-à-vis this 'communist' threat.

"It is that, of course, which leads to this tremendous—I consider it excessive—expenditure on military weapons. I think we pay a very, very heavy price for failing to deal more effectively with this East-West tension."

For McNamara, better East-West relations include a stronger Western Europe. "This should be one of our objectives for the 21st century," he says, "to help and encourage Europe to act in a more unified fashion.

"I think that today the West suffers because to a considerable degree it's fragmented. If we could reduce that fragmentation by assisting and encouraging Europe to unify itself—economically, politically, and certainly in terms of defense—we would be much better off."

With that, McNamara turns to the second major issue on his agenda: the population problem, brought sharply to his attention during his years at the World Bank.

While he acknowledges that some areas of the world face severe overcrowding, he says that "the problem today is not, on a global basis, density of population." What he describes as "the carrying capacity of the world"—the globe's capacity to support its population—is "greater than the existing world's population."

The problem arises instead from "the imbalance of population growth rates on the one hand and social and economic advance on the other"—which "leads to human misery."

"In sub-Saharan Africa as a whole," he says, "with the population of something on the order of 350 million people, food production growth rates—on average, per capita—have been *negative* for ten years.

"Now, ten years ago malnutrition existed, and if you have had a negative per-capita food production rate since that time, then there's less food per capita today than there was ten years ago.

"That kind of a situation is bound to have political repercussions—and it has had," he says, mentioning attempted coups as well as successive waves of migration. "And lest one think these migration problems are limited to Africa," he notes, "look at our own problem with Mexico."

There, he says, the problem arose from very high rates

of population growth several decades ago. The result is "a rate of increase in their labor force that is one of the highest in the world, roughly 3.2 percent per year.

"The Mexicans want to live in Mexico but the operative word is *live*. And if they can't live *there,* they're going to live *here,*" especially given the 2,000-mile-long U.S.–Mexican border that "cannot be protected no matter how much we expand the Immigration Service.

"I think we must recognize as a fact that for many purposes we are one market," he says, adding, "we have no choice but to take either their men or their goods."

In dealing with global population issues, McNamara sees two ways forward. One is to help nations reduce their population growth rates. In this regard, he says, better distribution of and education about contraceptives is part of the answer.

But he notes that "in many parts of East Africa where the population growth rates are 4 percent—which means that the population will double for those countries in seventeen years—the average woman during her reproductive years will produce eight children." And in many cases, he adds, "the women, when asked, state that they *want* six or seven children."

In such situations it's not enough to increase the availability of contraceptives. Instead, "one must change mind-sets."

Unless that change is made, McNamara warns, the resulting population growth will produce such serious "quality-of-life" problems for Bangladesh, India, and sub-Saharan African countries that their governments will be tempted to take "drastic action" to reduce population. The example of China's one-child-per-family policy, he says, suggests that such actions can be imposed only autocratically.

"I will predict that if those nations of East Africa do not

find a way to reduce the desired family size of seven or eight down toward two, they are going to move—certainly by the early part of the next century—to autocratic, repressive, dictatorial family systems that will restrict in the most brutal ways the size of families."

In that situation, he says, families may kill children whose presence would otherwise "place them above the prescribed limits of the state."

In addition to controlling population growth, McNamara sees a second way forward: an increase in the rate of economic development. In the 21st century, he says, the U.S. must contribute more to international economic development as an expression of the nation's traditional "concern for others" and "sense of compassion."

During the period of the Marshall Plan following World War II, when America's real income per capita was "less than half of what it is today," the nation was giving some 2.5 percent of its gross national product in foreign economic assistance. Today, he says, "we are spending on the order of [only] 0.21 percent of our GNP" for such assistance.

"I mention this because I think it shows a loss of sensitivity to our responsibility to others. It's a lack of compassion. It's a failure to pursue those values I felt we had traditionally respected in our society."

Part of the answer for developing nations, he says, is a direct transfer of resources from the industrial nations. But he feels it is even more important to "accelerate our own rate of economic advance because we are a market for their goods.

"It has become a truism to say that the world is becoming interdependent economically . . . our economic welfare depends on the welfare of Brazil, Mexico, India, and China, while their welfare depends on ours."

Finally, what about environmental degradation? McNamara ranks it as a serious problem, related in large part to the imbalance of population growth and economic development.

Despite a lack of certainty about the causes of certain environmental problems, such as acid rain, the destruction of the ozone layer, and the greenhouse effect, he says the developed nations should be "willing to buy insurance that will help us avoid undesirable, irreversible effects" by tackling what are thought to be the most likely causes of the problems.

"Later," he acknowledges, "it might prove that those were not the causes. In that case we would have wasted those funds.

"On the other hand, later it may prove that they *were* the causes, and we would have substantially reduced the cost" of battling the problem.

"But if we spent 1 or 2 or 3 percent of GNP to protect us against these uncertain environmental effects," he concludes, "I would suggest to you it's money well spent."

Global Science, Global Visions

IV

It's the lack of global vision that worries me, really. It's the issue of globalism that is missing in science.

—Abdus Salam

Abdus Salam

Freeman Dyson

Theodore J. Gordon

David Packard

Abdus Salam

Closing the Great Divide

One way or another, the economists in the previous section were deeply concerned not only about developments inside the Western nations but in the developing world as well. Looking over the parapet, Robert McNamara saw grave problems—not from population growth alone, but from the failure of the social and economic institutions to keep pace with birth rates. The world, he noted, has adequate "carrying capacity." But how will the 21st century cope with still-increasing levels of human misery across much of the globe?

The voices in this next section speak to that issue, and many others, through the language of science and technology. Abdus Salam, Freeman Dyson, Theodore Gordon, and David Packard bring the perspectives of physics, mathematics, aeronautical engineering, and electronic technology to bear on the next century. But their visions, in each case, extend far beyond their disciplines. Each is alive to the complexities that arise when modern science and advanced technologies come face to face with human needs, human foibles, and human politics. If the future they describe is sometimes heady, even fanciful, it is tempered throughout with a level-headed and sometimes sobering rationality. These are not, after all, creators of science fictions; each has made solid, tangible contributions to the world of scientific fact.

Leading the section is Pakistani physicist Abdus Salam, who speaks eloquently about the developing-world issues raised in the previous section. Ask the Nobel Prize-winner why he devotes so much of his energy to furthering the cause of science in the developing world, and he gives three reasons.

"You must realize first of all that I'm a Muslim," he says, adding, "for me the brotherhood of Muslims is a fundamental principal."

He notes, too, that his upbringing in a minority community in Pakistan gave him "a feeling for minorities." That very community, in fact, lined the streets of the country town of Jhang to applaud him in 1940 when, at age fourteen, he bicycled past after receiving the highest marks ever recorded on the entrance examination for Panjab University.

"The third thing is that I was exposed to the United Nations structure very early in my life," he says.

After attending Panjab University, Salam took his B.A. at St. John's College, Cambridge University. He received his Ph.D. in theoretical physics from Cambridge's Cavendish Laboratory and took an appointment, which he still holds, at Imperial College of Science and Technology in London. For his work in the physics of elementary particles—on which he has published some two hundred and fifty papers—he shared a Nobel Prize in 1979.

He now spends most of his time at the International Center for Theoretical Physics at Trieste, Italy, which he founded in 1964 and has directed ever since. In that capacity, and as head of the Third World Academy of Sciences, he has helped bring together physicists and mathematicians from the industrial nations and the developing world.

Trieste, Italy

The International Center for Theoretical Physics perches on a pine-covered slope overlooking the sapphire-blue Adriatic.

But the director's office looks out the back into the side of a hill. The location seems somehow in character for Abdus Salam, whose purpose lies less with elegant vistas than with little-known corners of the world—and who, despite his Nobel Prize for physics, typically describes himself as "a humble research physicist from a developing country."

Asked about his agenda for the next century, he responds without hesitation. "The real issue, to my mind," he says, "is the great divide between the South and the North," referring to those regions of the globe roughly representing the developing and the developed nations.

Although he speaks softly—from a desk chair facing a framed photograph of Albert Einstein and a blackboard chalked with mathematical formulas—his words carry fervor.

This "great divide" between the developing world and the industrial nations, he explains, arises from the fact that each side has a completely different set of problems. The major 21st-century issue facing the North, he says, is the arms race and the threat of nuclear warfare. The problem facing the South is the threat of starvation and utter poverty.

Picking up a copy of *Ideals and Realities,* a collection of his essays, he turns to a piece he wrote about Al Asuli, an 11th-century Islamic physician. Al Asuli, he says, divided the problems of humanity into diseases of the rich and diseases of the poor.

If Al Asuli were alive today, says Salam, he would make the same distinction. "Half his treatise would speak of the one affliction of rich humanity—the psychosis of nuclear annihilation. The other half would be concerned with the one affliction of the poor—their hunger and near-starvation. He might perhaps add that the two afflictions spring from a comon cause—the excess of science in one case and the lack of science in the other."

For Salam, the operative word here is *science*—which he is careful to distinguish from *technology*, or the application of scientific knowledge to human problems. One great difficulty for the developing world, he explains, is the misplaced assumption that sharing the latest in Western machinery, communications, and transportation—technology transfer—will be a panacea for the South.

"Technology transfer is something the South has asked for and the North is resisting. Quite rightly. I don't blame the North for one second for not giving technology as such. Why should you? Why should anybody part with things that nobody else has helped to create?"

"That's where the bread and butter is concerned," he adds, referring to the central role that the sale of technology plays in the economies of the industrial nations.

Instead of technology transfer, Salam says, the South in the coming century should be asking for a transfer of the basic science out of which technologies can spring. "I wish that the North could decide to give the South as much science as possible." Why this insistence on science? Because "science is the basis of technology in the present day." He cites the case of Japan. Over the years the Japanese invested heavily in learning "all of science at a very high level. And then they were really successful in their technology."

Similar things are beginning to happen, he says, in five of the developing nations: Argentina, Brazil, China, India, and South Korea. He is especially impressed by South Korea, which he recently visited.

"They took me straight away to the television studios for a two-hour-long interview," he recalls, "in which they said, 'We have made it a national objective to win Nobel prizes. Can you give us advice?'

"I told them they were being silly," he says with a chuckle, adding that "they may or may not get Nobel prizes." But he notes with approval that "the very fact that they made it a national objective is a very important thing. That means that they will stock up their libraries, they'll get scientific literature, they'll fund a lot of fellowships, they'll do everything possible to make themselves into a scientifically advanced country."

And that, he suggests, will do more for South Korea than any amount of reliance on Western technology.

As he looks forward into the 21st century, Salam distinguishes several kinds of science that will be practiced. The first he calls "science for science's sake"—the most basic and theoretical research, producing discoveries that sometimes go unappreciated for decades. In general such research is "probably in a healthy state," despite the never-ending battle to pay for it.

"Then there's science for man's sake," he says, a category he breaks down into three parts: "global science, science for the rich countries, and science for the poor countries."

"Science for the poor doesn't exist, simply doesn't exist," he laments—although he notes that the poor countries have plenty of problems that science could help resolve. He cites the current medical concern over AIDS: "As long as it remained in Haiti, nobody even bothered about it." Now that it has come to Europe and America, "it will get the attention it deserves."

"It always deserved that attention," he adds wryly.

And what about science for the rich countries? That gets entangled in defense spending—which, he says, accounts for half of all research spending in the developed world.

For Salam, in fact, the real threat of the nuclear arms race is not that it might end in holocaust. It is that swelling defense costs will sap resources needed to combat the rest of humanity's problems. It's a line of argument, he says, elaborated by President Dwight Eisenhower. "Eisenhower made it very clear that every single B-52 bomber that is made in America is depriving not only the poor in the third world but also Americans of sustenance, of shelter, of aid."

"If Eisenhower were alive, he would be just aghast" at current levels of defense spending and the lack of attention to the developing world. Referring to massive defense spending in the North on the one hand, and to developing-world poverty on the other, Salam drives home the connection. "Unless you are conscious that the two problems are connected, and that the developed nations are squandering the wealth of this world—not only the wealth of this world but also the time and the energies of its scientists and its technologists, which could be used toward bettering humanity—you'll never get to grips with" the basic challenge facing the 21st century.

But what about the peacetime spin-offs that arise from defense-based research? "The statement that defense expenditures have 'fallout' is rubbish, total rubbish," Salam says flatly. "And the statement that since you invest in 'star wars' you will do your toothpaste better is also total rubbish."

What's really needed, he says, is not the "fallout" from defense projects but a concentrated effort to study some of the developing world's most pressing problems—starvation, for example. Although he supports the idea of food aid for developing nations, he sees it as only a "short-term business." The root of the problem is "food deficiency, drought, and desertification."

"This is the basic problem to be solved scientifically." But across much of the developing world, he points out, "there are no scientific studies at all of climate and of the underground water situation in the deserts—whether there are underground lakes, and so on." The lack of such studies, which are common enough in the developed countries, supports his contention that "science for the rich" is something quite different from "science for the poor."

One problem in conducting such studies, however, is that they frequently transcend national boundaries.

For that reason, they fall under Salam's third heading of "global science"—the study of the largest interdisciplinary and international issues concerning the global environment.

On this point, he expresses profound pessimism. "There's no such thing as global science as a subject," he complains. Even the disappearance of rain forests, which is commanding increased public attention, is not being considered in global terms.

"People do not take the rain forest as a global asset," he laments. "People take it as a problem of Brazil, a problem of Malaysia. How many governments are willing to spend money on that sort of thing? None. Zero." The problem is the lack of "the scientific infrastructure to look at the global problems."

"Everybody seems to be for himself," he says sadly. "There is no global vision at all. It's the lack of global vision that worries me, really. It's the issue of globalism that is missing in science, that is missing in the food problem, that is missing in the health problem." What is needed is "a vision of a sort that I don't see any statesman having."

From his position as an administrator, Salam says he clearly sees the need for sources of funding that would encourage such globalism. He adds that such funds, if they are to come, will have to come from the developed world.

But he again rejects as "rubbish"—one of his favorite words—the idea that "if you save funds from nuclear arms limitation you will put them into the welfare of mankind." The temptation, he says, will be for the rich countries simply to funnel the savings back into tax relief—"making the rich richer and the poor hungry man's soul sink lower."

"The whole attitude has to become very different."

And if the "great divide" between the rich and poor nations is not closed? Salam says that it will be increasingly "hard to ignore the developing countries' problems in the 21st century" for two reasons.

First, he says, the North will no longer be able to "insulate itself" politically from the South. If the gap is not narrowed, "what will happen is what is happening already in the third world"—turmoil, military governments, unrest, and "people on top of each other."

Second, he notes that the worldwide environment "may be affected by lack of attention to the global problems and to scientific globalism."

"In that sense, no parts of the world are going to be safe from the feeling of turmoil. At the moment, it doesn't seem to affect Americans to have starving Africans at their hands. They may very well say, 'Well, if they want to starve, let them starve.' "

"But I don't think man lives like this," he says. Speaking of rock star Bob Geldof's efforts to raise money for African famine relief, he says, "I think the Geldofs of this world make their point when they show what can be done in a small way."

What, then, does he hope will close the gap? He would like to see industrial nations "specialize" in providing the scientific training to elevate the developing nations. "For example, higher education may be taken up by Britain and the United States. The Russians may take up lower education. The Japanese and the Germans will be asked to do technology."

"That," he concludes, "will be my vision of the future."

Freeman Dyson

Colonizing the Universe

Freeman Dyson's career doesn't fit the usual pigeonholes. A British theoretical physicist who has admitted to being "obsessed with the future," he's comfortable in the fields of nuclear physics, rocket technology, and astrophysics as well. A naturalized United States citizen whose opinions are sought in American military circles, he nevertheless takes an active role in peace movements. The designer of a nuclear-powered starship, he is also the author of two well-received books, Disturbing the Universe *(1979) and* Weapons and Hope *(1984), both written with considerable skill and grace.*

"I didn't once take a course in physics in school," he says. "The important thing was that I had a home background that encouraged me to go ahead and just get into sciences and do something."

He was born in England to a well-known musician and educator, Sir George Dyson, and Mildred Lucy Dyson, a lawyer. He taught himself calculus at age fifteen by studying a textbook over Christmas break. After World War II, during which he served in operations research with the Royal Air Force Bomber Command, he completed his degree in mathematics at Trinity College, Cambridge, and pursued further work at Cornell University. While still in his twenties, he was instrumental in refining the theory of quantum electrodynamics. Since 1953 he has been a professor of physics at the Institute for Advanced Study in Princeton.

A long-time proponent of space colonization, he thinks of himself as a modern-day Richard Hakluyt, the 16th-century Oxford geography professor who championed England's colonizing effort in the Americas. "He never went to any of these places," says Dyson. "He just preached. And in the end people listened."

"If I have a role," Dyson adds, "it's the role of Hakluyt."

Princeton, New Jersey

The issue of energy rises toward the top of many agendas for the 21st century. It doesn't even make it onto Freeman Dyson's list. "I don't regard that as a real problem," says Dyson, with the chuckle of a man who knows all sorts of wonderful secrets and who is eager to spring them upon the unwary.

"If you have advanced biotechnology, I don't see any difficulty in getting all the energy you want from the sun," he explains. "It's only a question of redesigning trees so that they produce something other than wood. Gasoline, for example. Alcohol. Convenient fuels."

You mean, he is asked, you would get fuel the way you get sap from a sugar maple—by tapping the tree?

"I wouldn't do it so crudely," he says. "I would have a sort of living, underground pipeline system, so that the gasoline would be delivered where you want it."

Direct from the tree, with no refining?

"Why not?" he replies. "All those things I think will be available in at the most fifty years—looking at the ways the [genetic] technology is going."

It's the kind of thinking that for years has flowed from this small, second-floor office overlooking the quiet lawns of the Institute for Advanced Study. Dyson, a slender man sitting with his back to the window, takes a refreshingly unfamiliar perspective on the world's problems.

"I take a long view of things," he admits. "I find it

difficult to discuss . . . day-to-day events, because I'm looking to another century."

As the author of *Weapons and Hope,* a book setting out the possibilities for dialogue between the military establishment and the peace movement (both of which he knows firsthand), he naturally puts the problem of nuclear weaponry high on his agenda. He notes, however, that "I have nothing new to say" on the subject.

Instead, he turns to a handful of other issues that he feels will demand particular attention in the next century, including biotechnology, space, population, education, and class distinctions.

Central to Dyson's vision of the future is the use of biotechnology as a means of creating environments that are not only productive but pleasant.

Designing plants—like the gasoline-producing trees— "will be a new art form," he says, in which the designers will strive "to make them not only useful but also beautiful and clean and elegant."

Lest his listeners imagine, however, that his purpose is simply to enrich the earth's resources, Dyson makes it clear that his heart is elsewhere. His real goal: the colonization of space, which he is convinced will happen during the 21st century.

The planet earth, he says, "is clearly in considerable dangers of all sorts. The question is . . . whether you may reduce the risks to life by spreading it out more widely into space."

Asked to elaborate on the dangers to the earth, he answers bluntly.

"*We* are the risks. We're the ones who are destroying life on the planet. Essentially, the problem is to remove the destructive effects of our species on all the others."

"You're not going to solve that problem by colonizing the other planets," he concedes. "But you may alleviate it."

Such colonization, however, may not come in the forms envisioned by popular literature—either by finding life already existent in space, or by sending human beings out to live in what he calls the "tin cans" of man-made, expensive, unaesthetic space stations.

Nor, he says, is a colony likely to be established on another planet. Dyson's goal, instead, is to find a solid, sunny chunk of celestial real estate—perhaps one of the numerous asteroids that orbit between Mars and Jupiter—and create an environment that would eventually be able to support human life. He's not overly concerned about the lack of water, nor even by the absence of an atmosphere. That's where biotechnology enters. He foresees that plants will be designed that can grow little "greenhouses" around themselves and generate their own atmospheres—a development that leads him to speak fondly of a yet-to-be-invented tuber he calls the "Martian potato."

Dyson is convinced, then, that technology will not stand in the way of colonizing space. But will there be sufficient human motivation? Here he points to another of the major agenda items for the 21st century: the issue of population.

"The human species on earth has got to be submitting itself to all kinds of disciplines in order to survive," he says. One of the foremost is the discipline of controlling population.

So far, Dyson suggests, the earth is not hopelessly overcrowded.

"You can live a civilized life with a much higher population density than we have in the United States," he says, singling out the densely populated Netherlands as "a very civilized country" in which "the countryside looks beautiful."

But he adds that the world "can't go on growing at the present rate for very long . . . somewhere you're going to really hit the stops." Those stops have already been reached, he notes, in China, where government regulations are aimed at permitting only one child per couple.

"That's tough," Dyson says. "I have six kids, and I would hate to be limited to one." But he feels strongly that "that's the kind of discipline we're going to have to live under in order to preserve this planet."

Such imposed limits, he says, may well provide one of the motivations for colonizing space—just as they sometimes provide, on earth, an impetus for immigration.

"The point about immigration," he explains, "is not that it really reduces the population substantially. But at least it makes the severe discipline more acceptable, if the people who really rebel can go off somewhere else." As on earth, he suggests, so in space—where colonization, especially at the outset, may provide a means whereby "people who really can't take it can leave."

Dyson foresees that the strongest push for space colonization, in fact, will be made by the very people who do want to "go off somewhere else," and who will thrust into space in fairly small, private-enterprise ventures.

"The governments, of course, are going to continue exploring," he says, noting the success of such operations as the *Voyager 2* probe that passed Uranus in January 1986. "Governments can do that kind of thing very well. What I don't think the governments are good at is organizing human settlements. That, I would hope, will be done by the people themselves, so they can do it the way they want to."

What about the expense? "I think there is a great deal of illusion in that.

"The really good space exploring wasn't that expensive. Things that cost the most money are usually the least productive scientifically. You don't need vast sums of money. You just need to be clever.

"I'm not saying the government shouldn't support science," he hastens to add. "Obviously it should." But, he says, "I never expected much from the government, anyway."

It's a point that leads Dyson, as he contemplates the future, to shy away from programs that depend heavily on government involvement. "I regard governments as a necessary evil; I don't expect any sort of perfection from a government.

"They muddle along, and that's all you can say. I wouldn't want to have the government intruding more than it does. I'm sort of a Reaganite at heart, I suppose: I believe that the less government the better."

Then would Dyson, like some other forward-looking thinkers, want to see some form of world federal government?

"No, on the contrary," he responds, with some alarm. "That would be terrible." Fortunately, he says, the power of governments tends to diminish over long distances—providing a kind of self-limiting factor on the geographical extent of any governing body.

"That's a happy state of affairs," he says. "I think it's a good thing the world has more countries now than it had when I grew up. . . . Small countries on the whole are socially better run than big ones." The United States, he notes, is "evidently too big, and I think that's probably the cause of most of our problems."

Dyson takes an uncommon perspective on still another item on his agenda for the future—the educational system. Far from calling for a widespread and centralized movement for education reform, he says he remains "quite impressed with the advantages of *not* having a well-organized system" of education. What he looks for, instead, is a means of fostering real creativity in students.

"There is something lacking in modern life," he notes. "One of the reasons I'd like to go to Mars or some other place is simply to find the peace and quiet that used to be on earth." That peace, he says, is an essential element in the creative process. "In the old times you'd go through a wet Sunday and have absolutely nothing to do," he recalls. "That forced you to think." A rainy climate "produced a lot of the creativity in northern Europe."

Dyson's goal is an educational system that "gives the kids a lot more flexibility." He objects to the educational structures in the "well-organized" European countries, where "the kids are under terrible pressure." And he particularly disapproves of the French system, in which students "have to do the *baccalauréat* that determines their fate for the rest of their lives."

He admires, instead, the "tremendous looseness in the structure" in U.S. education. "If you don't get into one college, you get into another, and in the end it doesn't really matter whether it was Harvard or not." Having spoken recently at several small, little-known colleges in New Jersey, he says he has been impressed with the brightness of the students he has encountered.

The bulk of his concern about education focuses on the postgraduate level. His remedy? "First of all, abolish the Ph.D. system."

Especially in the sciences, he says, "the educational system is designed to drag out the time it takes to get qualifications. But you don't need all that. The best work I did was at a time when I was tremendously ignorant. You don't want to stuff your head full. . . . That's why I'm against the Ph.D. system: It slows people down tremendously and quite unnecessarily. Only the very best are able to withstand it.

"I don't have a Ph.D. myself, and I never produced Ph.D.'s. The teaching I do is strictly outside the system."

What would he do in place of the Ph.D.? "Simply let people loose and give them a Ph.D. at birth," he says, breaking into his slightly elfin grin, "and then let them get on with their education."

The suggestion may be partly in jest. But it flows from Dyson's altogether serious perception of yet another item on the 21st century's agenda: the increasing problem of class distinction.

"One of the things I see as very bad is the accentuating split between the educated and the uneducated." He recalls the relief he felt when, on first coming to America from England, he found he could talk to cabdrivers "without being immediately identified as upper class."

Now, he says, "the class system in this country is getting more rigid. And it's largely a result of this elitist educational apparatus." He is especially concerned about a tendency to require what he calls "papers," or credentials. "For every kind of administrative job, you're supposed to have an M.B.A. or something." As a result, "the people who manage and the people who teach are sort of becoming a hereditary caste."

Finally, what about the raising of the children who will someday participate in the educational process?

"I wouldn't force anybody to raise kids," says Dyson, whose five working daughters have so far elected not to raise families. "I think it's a vocation. I think the ideal society is probably one where one family out of three has six kids, and the rest have zero."

That way, he adds, "only those with a real vocation for it raise families. And they do it with love and a great deal of care."

Theodore J. Gordon

Better Mousetrapping, Better Ideas

To solve today's problems, Theodore J. Gordon turns to the future.

"Solutions can't all be based on what happened in the past," he says. "If you take a projection from history and extrapolate it, it's got to be wrong, because there are new things about the future that will change that extrapolation."

In 1965, as an engineer at the McDonnell Douglas Astronautics Company, he wrote a book titled The Future—*"on the theory that at least a component of the future could be described on the basis of research in progress today."*

"I was fascinated by it," he says, "but I was doing it as an amateur." That book put him in contact with several researchers at the RAND Corporation, with whom he established the nonprofit Institute for the Future in Middletown, Connecticut, in 1968. In 1971 he left to found the Futures Group, a private consulting firm that does the bulk of its work under government contract.

After graduating with a bachelor of science degree from Louisiana State University in 1950, Gordon earned a master of science degree in aerodynamics at Georgia Institute of Technology in 1951. In his sixteen years at McDonnell Douglas, he served as chief engineer for the Saturn program, test conductor at Cape Canaveral for the Thor rocket, and director of advanced space systems and launch vehicles. He has written and collaborated on a number of book, holds several patents, and has produced more than one hundred reports at the Futures Group on topics ranging from geothermal energy to the future consumption of soft drinks.

Glastonbury, Connecticut

On Ted Gordon's desk sits a white model of a Thor rocket. On his walls are photographs of gliders. And on his agenda for the 21st century are flights of technological inventiveness that could both resolve and complicate the problems facing mankind.

As he settles into his chair for the interview, the former aerospace engineer admits with a smile that "I'll be talking about a technological future that's all glitter and better mousetrapping." His ideas, however, are not merely speculative. Anchoring his vision of the future in the long-term forecasting done by his seventy-member, sixteen-year-old consulting firm, he begins with the ongoing computer revolution.

"The trends that we see in making computers smaller, faster, cheaper seem to have in them the seeds of another two decades of growth," he says.

The result: computers with ten thousand times the current capability within twenty to thirty years. "That means machines on the desk that can do what main frames do today, with storage capabilities of staggering proportions."

What will be the consequences of these developments? "In the old days we worried about computers forcing us into a mold," he says. "The concern was that we would be regimented.

"I think quite the opposite is the result." The new technology, he says, will actually encourage individuality.

To illustrate, he describes an experimental promotion undertaken by Chevrolet. It consisted of a disk allowing users of personal computers to assemble, on their screen, the truck they wanted from a vast list of options, and then determine its performance standards, calculate its cost, and test drive it around a simulated track.

Shoppers, Gordon notes, will be able to use computers to assemble such preprogrammed options "in the way that is most meaningful to the individual." Thus computers will "promote individuality of choice and diversity."

New computers will also help "equalize small business and large business." In the past, the capacity to handle information differentiated large and small businesses. In the future, "that threshold will be lowered."

Education, too, will be affected. In the near term, he says, some textbooks will be accompanied by computer disks providing data bases and models that will help students investigate the subject.

Further out in the 21st century, he sees computer simulation as "an exceedingly important educational tool." So far, he says, it has been applied only to such areas as pilot training.

But imagine computer simulations that teach labor-management negotiations. "You can play Continental Illinois," he says, "and see if you can pull the corporation out of the tailspin. But it's not just a computer game. You are there across the table from this three-dimensional image that is negotiating with you. You're playing chess, but human chess here in a realistic situation."

In such simulations "you are learning in a way that doesn't require your being taught. The learning goes on because you're being subjected to a realistic environment."

Other major advances are also on his horizon.

Genetics "I can't overemphasize the importance of this frontier." The next century will see the widespread use of microorganisms to produce specific chemicals. And genetic research may also allow the reading of "the genome," the complete set of chromosomes for an individual plant or animal. By reading the genetic code of a human infant or adult, for example, "you'll be able to tell everything about that person that is genetically determined"—including a hereditary propensity for certain diseases.

Once people read their own genetic "books," he says, "there will be an overwhelming need to manipulate [the genes and] to cure before the disease occurs—to change fate to the degree that the genetic molecule projects fate."

Will we, then, deliberately try to build in traits from the start? "I suspect so," he answers. "For example, if we consider low intelligence to be undesirable, and we have the ability to manipulate the gene in embryo to improve intelligence, wouldn't we do it? The capability for doing that by the year 2100 is a fair bet, maybe well before that." But couldn't one also manipulate to produce *low* intelligence—to create a slave race, for example? Admitting the possibility, he notes that the entire issue has "got a lot of hellish overtones to it."

Psychology "I think we're on the verge of a breakthrough in the understanding of how the brain functions"—a breakthrough that has both "scary consequences and important and favorable consequences."

The real question, says Gordon, is the nature of memory. If it turns out to be chemical, the use of "psychotropic" or mind-modifying drugs to increase, alter, or erase memory is conceivable. "That means that the ability to create moods and tailor performance—even transmit information chemically—has to be imagined."

By 2030, he foresees that drugs may be developed that will produce "certain predictable mental states that will be seen to be desirable." He mentions drugs to improve attention spans, to produce "programmed dreams . . . where the dream is a predictable one," and even "programmed attitudes with respect to war" or "population control through the control of basic human drives."

Artificial Intelligence Of particular interest to Gordon is the development of "artificial expertise," in which a computer, fed by "the judgments of experts responding to particular problems," will create its own expert decision-making system—and even be capable of learning from its mistakes.

"The interesting thing about this approach," he says, is that "the judgments of various people who are expert at different disciplines can be combined, so that the synthetic expert that's created has ostensibly the experience levels of all of the people who contribute to its construction." In theory, "the machine becomes better than any single expert."

Robotics Combining the developments of artificial intelligence, miniaturization, and manipulation, the coming generations of robots should respond even to unfamiliar environments and strange situations.

"I think what comes out of this, in the near term, is a series of household robots." These will not be "little R2-D2s," he explains, referring to the robot character in the *Star Wars* movies; instead, they will be machines for special-purpose jobs.

"Snow-eaters are my favorite example. On a snowy morning, you send them out to the driveway, they eat the snow, and they park back in the garage and recharge their batteries."

But robots raise serious threats—especially when used in place of people on production lines.

"Our studies here show that between now and the turn of the century, robotics and further automation will not have the capability, on the whole, of replacing the large percentage of the labor force." But certain industries, like automobile manufacturing, could be hit much harder.

"Beyond the turn of the century, however, it's much less clear that the overall impact will be benign," he says. "We can talk about machines replacing labor and resulting in large-scale unemployment and catastrophe, or machines replacing labor resulting in much-needed increases in human understanding and leisure and enjoyment."

Space Gordon foresees increasing work on space stations. By mid-century, "manned exploration of the solar system" may well become "a unifying goal, maybe an international goal."

"From the platform of 2050, we'll look back and wonder why we stopped when we had won the moon." Manned exploration "still has the ability to fire imaginations."

He does not, however, foresee much business being carried on in space.

"Every time we've looked at the economics of manufacture in space, it's proven to be illusive." But he sees one possible use: waste disposal—by rocketing noxious materials straight into the sun, "the ultimate disposal."

Aging Already, says Gordon, increasing numbers of people are living into their nineties—although few are living past one hundred. Toward the end of the next century, however, "we can begin to conjecture that the number of people who will be much older than the oldest people today" will increase. But that will happen only if technology solves "the riddle of aging."

Gordon also points to future developments in several other technologies. One is the science of materials, particularly the recent breakthrough in superconductors of electricity that do not require temperatures as cold as their predecessors. "That's phenomenally important in terms of improved efficiency of motors, for example" or for building "light bulbs that store their own energy."

Another area is micromechanics. Using the techniques of photolithography to create extremely small machines, he says, allows the construction of "pipes, valves, pumps, even rotating machinery" measuring only one-eighth of an inch or less.

Such machines could be used as "little transmitters built into concrete buildings so that they can telemeter stress after an earthquake." Also possible: electronic listening devices or "bugs" the size of a grain of salt.

What can technology contribute to solving the major problems facing mankind in the 21st century?

Noting that superpower arms-control treaties are difficult because "we [in the United States] don't trust them [in the Soviet Union] and they don't trust us," he points to the need for "a technology of treaty violation detection." One way forward is to "take these ultrasmall machines and build them into whatever it is they're building"—to transmit data directly to watchdog organizations.

On the population issue, Gordon points to the need for better food production for a world that will have 10 billion inhabitants in the next century. Needed, he says, is "the complete revision of agriculture as we've known it."

In the past "we've always *grown* food" rather than manufacturing it. But with the advances in genetics "you can think about things like steak factories, where cells are produced and instructed to self-replicate, or triggered into self-replication, to produce material that can then be transformed and consumed by human beings. In other words, we will not necessarily be tied to land for production."

On the question of the "North-South gap" between the developed and the developing worlds, Gordon is less sanguine. He sees the gap widening because of technology—since industrial-world technologies are aimed at saving labor, while the developing world needs to find ways to employ increasing populations. In trying to use modern production technologies, for example, developing countries increase their output at the expense of jobs and thereby "create the potential for political instability."

"I'm not giving you 'small is beautiful,' " he adds. "What I am saying is that there is a whole class of technology not yet discovered that may be big technology, but it is labor-intensive."

Finally, on the question of public and private morality, Gordon observes that "technology can only challenge morality, because it provides new domains in which old moral issues must be tested.

"I used to say that values are built on a framework that technology creates, and people will do whatever they're capable of doing and then bend the morality to justify it. I no longer believe that. But it's not entirely false."

In fact, he feels that in the relation of morality to technology the latter will tend to dominate. "Where the technology provides the capability to do something that is economically desired, then the morality adapts. I think that's true—more true than the converse, which is that we won't develop the technology if it's morally repugnant.

"We may have some technology-free zones," he concludes, "but the world thrust is in the opposite direction."

David Packard

Common Problems, Common Sense

"The most important thing about my career," says multimillionaire David Packard, cofounder of the Hewlett-Packard Company, is that "I decided I wanted to be an engineer when I was about ten years old and never changed."

Raised in Colorado and educated at Stanford University, Packard recalls doing an undergraduate independent-study course on the history of the westward movement across America. "I remember thinking at the time," he chuckles, "that I was born too late, that I missed all the opportunities."

He was clearly wrong. With college classmate William R. Hewlett and $538 in capital, he began tinkering in his garage in California, inventing such things as an electronic harmonica tuner and a bowling alley foul-line indicator. When Walt Disney ordered eight audio-oscillators for the sound track of Fantasia, *the company that would become the world's largest producer of electronic measuring instruments and a major computer manufacturer was off and running.*

In 1969 Packard, a Republican, joined the Nixon administration as deputy secretary of defense, a position he held until 1971. More recently, he has chaired two committees convened by the Reagan administration: the so-called Packard Commission, which released its report on the nation's defense management in 1986, and a panel of the White House Science Council, which reported on the health of the nation's colleges and universities.

Giving heavily of his time to public-service activities, he has been a member of the Palo Alto School Board, held numerous academic trusteeships, and been showered with awards by organizations ranging from the Electronic Industries Association to the Natural Resources Defense Council and the Boy Scouts.

New York

Offering his visitor the hotel room's only armchair, David Packard takes the straight-backed chair beside the bed—which, at nine in the morning, is already made. Gracious, unpretentious, he brings an engineer's sense of order and reasonableness to his life, in everything from his personal relationships to his thinking about the next century's agenda.

"I think that we must find some way to get more common sense, more rationality, in our decisions," he says, "and less emotion."

It is a conviction that, like a musical theme, returns again and again throughout the ninety-minute interview.

"We are reaching the point where every country in the world is affected by the global situation," he observes. As a result, "the major countries are going to have to deal with all of their affairs on a global basis."

What, to Packard, are the major global issues? "The most important question we have to deal with," he begins, "is a combination of population control and the control of our environment—how to utilize the world in as effective a way as we can for the future of mankind.

"Anytime you look at the long-range situation, you come to the conclusion that, unless we can limit the population, the other problems are eventually going to become unmanageable."

He sees the population-growth problem as most

acute in the developing nations, particularly those in Africa and South America, where "population just outstrips the resources."

How can the problem be confronted? The answer, he acknowledges, is complex. But in part it involves being "more rational about birth control and abortion," topics that sometimes "get very emotional."

"While population growth may not be a short-term danger, I think in the long term that it's going to make our job of trying to provide leadership toward a better world much more difficult.

"The United States certainly should be a leader in helping with this problem," he concludes, adding that "it has not been as high on our agenda as I think it should have been."

Equally high on his agenda is the issue of the worldwide degradation of the natural environment. "The environment is going to determine, in the final analysis, what population can be supported."

In this area, "there's a lot that can be done. It ranges all the way from trying to preserve some attractive examples of ecology—so that you can keep some of the original character of our country and countries around the world—on down to questions of food production and the preservation of farmland."

The greatest danger to the environment, he feels, arises from intensive farming: loss of topsoil through erosion, the disappearance of forests through land clearing and harvesting firewood, and toxic pollution through the use of insecticides and fertilizers.

But Packard is concerned, too, about atmospheric pollution and its apparent effect on the ozone layer. "We're changing the character of the atmosphere, which might change the average temperature of our planet." The result could be "some very drastic changes in the climate."

Both population growth and environmental degradation, he notes, "are problems that develop slowly, that are difficult to detect, and that are difficult to assess for the long-term outcome.

"I don't think these problems will get to a very critical point in the 21st century," he adds, noting that it will probably take "a longer time period for those kinds of things to have any serious impact."

Then why put these twin problems at the head of the list? Because he sees a need to deal with them before they get out of hand. "This country deals with problems only when they begin to approach a crisis stage," says Packard, much of whose career has been spent working in and with the public sector. "When they're not in a crisis stage, no one pays any attention to them."

A third point commanding his attention is the issue of the world's energy supplies. For Packard, the energy question is closely related to his first two agenda items: As growing populations develop greater needs for energy, the search for and consumption of energy supplies puts additional pressure on the environment.

In recent years, he says, "We've had a recess in the energy crisis," but he believes that phenomenon is short-lived. "It probably won't last until the beginning of the 21st century." After that, he continues, "I think we'll face a serious crisis in oil and natural gas."

Coal is not the answer, since it pollutes the atmosphere, produces ash that must be dumped, and causes a "horrendous" transportation problem.

Where, then, will the 21st century's energy come from?

"Unfortunately, the best option we have right now is nuclear energy"—which, particularly in the United States, "has been affected so much by emotional reactions that it has not been acceptable.

"I don't think the people who were involved [in nuclear power generation] in the early days recognized how serious the safety and reliability problems were. But in my opinion, those can be dealt with in a perfectly satisfactory manner."

He thinks that in the very long run, nuclear fusion may be promising, although researchers are now "just barely to the point of being able to make it work" and have yet to find "a very practical way of using the energy" released by fusion.

But whether by fusion of fission, "in my view, we're going to have to come to some form of nuclear power sooner or later—and I would think that we'll have to do that during the 21st century."

And that leads Packard directly into a fourth item he is eager to put on the agenda: the faltering support of scientific education and research, not only in America but worldwide.

"The universities have been the prime source of new science from their work in basic research, and at the same time they are also the producers of scientific talent for the future," says Packard, who for the last four years has chaired the Panel on the Health of U.S. Colleges and Universities convened by the White House Science Council.

When the panel published its final report, it concluded that "the federal support that has been provided during the last decade or so has not been adequate to keep the resources of the universities up to the responsibility we expect of them." One reason: the increasing expense of equipment as the frontiers of science move ahead.

"When I first started in the electronics field forty years ago, a few hundred dollars' worth of instrumentation was all you needed to do some research or development. Today, you can't work at the frontiers of technology and electronics without equipment costing millions of dollars."

Part of the problem has been that funds that might have gone to university research have been put elsewhere.

"Despite the fact that the federal government has provided a very large level of support for science, we do not have a rational national policy on research and development." Lacking such a policy, "our government tends to support things that are glamorous but don't contribute very much to the solution of basic problems."

One example is the expensive space-shuttle program. "A comparable amount of research on materials might have been much more important to the economy and maybe to the welfare of the society.

"It's time that we developed some means of utilizing our best scientific talent in the country for planning rational programs," he asserts.

As scientific research becomes increasingly global in scope, however, the need for multinational support becomes apparent. And that leads Packard to the next item on his agenda: the economic relations among nations.

"Without any question there's going to be a basic change in the balance of the global economies. It's very hard to predict how that's going to come out." As Japan and other Asian nations rise, Europe may well continue "slipping still further." But "the more serious problem" is "whether the United States is going to be able to maintain its leadership in technology and in other areas."

As the U.S. economy shifts from heavy industry to high-technology and service-sector businesses, the country will continue to move out of "a period when natural resources were the key to a strong economy" and into a period in which "you don't need any particular resources except the education of your people."

As that shift occurs, "a wave of protectionism" could sweep across the world as nations strive to retain traditional markets. That, says Packard, could be "disastrous," noting that "the only option we have is to work toward developing the United States to deal in a world economy rather than a domestic economy."

And that means dealing with the Soviets as well. "One of the very important challenges for the 21st century is for the United States and the Soviet Union to develop a better accommodation, a better working relationship," he says. "I don't see how the world can continue unless we can somehow find ways of working together."

He does not mean "anything like unilateral disarmament." His point is simply that the current pitch of defense spending in both countries has produced what he calls "a completely unnatural situation," draining resources needed elsewhere.

"I think we've got to recognize that these problems should be solved on the basis of the self-interests of the countries involved." The Soviet Union, he says, needs a closer relationship with the United States because the Soviet Union lags in science, technology, agriculture, and other areas. Likewise, he notes, the Soviet Union and the East-bloc nations could "provide a very large market" for U.S. products.

Such "accommodation" is "an area of great opportunity that is likely to develop in the 21st century. And if that *could* develop, that could assure a century of peace."

What about the danger of nuclear war? Unlike many future-minded thinkers, Packard thinks that this threat is "very low at this time." He notes that both superpowers "understand the potential dangers of an all-out nuclear war," and that communications between the two are good enough to prevent an "accidental occurrence" that could lead to war.

On the subject of international debt—another issue appearing on a number of 21st-century agendas—Packard is not unduly concerned. "I see that as a transient problem rather than a permanent one."

Far more pressing, especially in the United States, are

what he calls "the pressures of the stock market that encourage management to focus on short-term gains rather than the long-term prosperity of a company.

"I don't see any signs that this is clearing up," he says, noting that "It will get worse before it gets better."

Finally, in Packard's own field of communications technology, he foresees no new developments that will "revolutionize" communications the way solid-state, digital, and satellite technology have already done.

"I think we now have a gap in what we're communicating *about* rather than what we're communicating *with*." Current television programming, he notes, has "certainly not been very rational as far as young people are concerned.

"I hope that the next century may provide a revolution in *how* we communicate, using the technology that we already have."

A World Made of Grace

V

The world is made of grace, and the important thing is to understand that . . . we are all struggling between values.
—Carlos Fuentes

Lloyd Richards

Andrei Voznesensky

Carlos Fuentes

Lloyd Richards

Fitting It All Together

Science and technology have given us astonishing new channels of communication. But they have not, as David Packard suggested at the end of the previous section, told us how to talk to one another. That subject—how we tell each other who we are, what we are doing here, and why we must go on—is properly the province of the arts.

On the surface, the three artists speaking in this section seem to have little in common. They belong to different cultures. They hail from different geopolitical divisions of the world. They practice different arts. Yet Lloyd Richards, Andrei Voznesensky, and Carlos Fuentes have a common commitment to the future of the arts— not simply for the sake of the arts, but for the health, the vitality, and even the survivability of the future. For them, the arts are not peripheral luxuries or disposable occupations, readily left behind as the future unrolls. They are essential ingredients in a world moving ever more rapidly forward and wondering, as it goes, what it all means.

"There is no easy path for anyone in the arts," says actor-director Lloyd Richards, who opens this section. His own path has brought him to America's top post in theater education: dean of the Yale School of Drama and artistic director of the Yale Repertory Theater. But it hasn't always been easy.

Born in Toronto, son of a carpenter, Richards grew up in Detroit and studied at Wayne State University. After serving in the United States Army Air Force during World War II, he spent several years as a disk jockey in Detroit before taking up acting in New York. There he spent two years on a radio serial, "Hotel for Pets," appeared on television shows ranging from "Hallmark Hall of Fame" to "The Guiding Light," and played various roles in Off Broadway and Broadway productions.

After several directing stints with Michigan theaters, Richards became the first black director on Broadway when, in 1959, he directed Sidney Poitier in A Raisin in the Sun. *Since then, he has directed several other Broadway plays, including* Paul Robeson *with James Earl Jones. He also directed a segment of Alex Haley's television series, "Roots."*

Keenly interested in art that addresses profound subjects, Richards is in the forefront of the search for new plays. "I can understand people becoming frustrated by solutions that don't solve," says Richards, who since 1969 has been artistic director of the nation's most important workshop for new plays, the National Playwrights Conference at the O'Neill Theater Center.

"I think we would all like to know that there are answers and it will all fit together—and we can make it fit together. I think that's why we go on."

New Haven, Connecticut

On one level, Lloyd Richards's concerns about the 21st century are perfectly predictable. He asks the question on the minds of arts administrators everywhere: How do we ensure the prosperity, or even the survival, of the arts in the future?

On another level, however, the dean of the Yale School of Drama has a far more profound concern. It hovers over everything he says in his softly modulated and serious voice. It pulses through the playbills covering his walls and the books strewn on his shelves. When it condenses into words—

A World Made of Grace 142

as it does, more than once, during an hour-long interview in his modest, somewhat disorganized office—it takes the form of questions about the fundamental purpose of artistic expression: What is the meaning of modern life, and how do the arts help us understand it?

For Richards, the two levels are tightly interwoven. Troubled by the economic difficulties facing many artists, he illustrates his concern by recalling a time when, traveling to various parts of the country, he ran into one of the nation's finest theatrical set designers at airport after airport.

"Each time he was carrying a model of a different set— a major artist who was running around with four sets for four theaters. Why? To try and make a living, because he had a couple of kids that he would like to send to college.

"Is that what he should have been doing?" Richards muses. Was humanity "getting the best out of him"?

And are we, in general, "getting the best that we can from our artists?" he asks.

"That's what the 21st century must address," he asserts.

Why is that such a pressing issue? Why is it essential that humanity get "the best" from its artists?

The answer for him doesn't lie in some vague art-for-art's-sake notion. Nor is he merely speaking as an insider trying to defend his turf.

For Richards, art is simply integral to humanity. As the items on mankind's agenda become increasingly challenging—items that, for him, include nuclear warfare, environmental pollution, the possible destruction of the planet, and the colonization of space—so the role of the arts becomes increasingly important.

"The arts, for me, have always been something that brought perspective to events—that *illuminated,* not just *represented,* the moment." The purpose of the arts, he explains, is not so much to portray reality as to bring "an insight" into the significance of events.

That's not a new purpose, he insists, noting that the arts have always had that "responsibility." He observes that whenever society encountered monumental changes—the human use of fire, the invention of the wheel, the discovery that the world is round—the role of the arts has been to examine "how such developments changed and really revolutionized a society."

What is new, Richards believes, is the nature of the threats now facing mankind and, therefore, the nature of the subjects that the arts of the 21st century must confront.

The most serious threat he sees is the danger of nuclear annihilation—and the mental consequences of that threat. "Once you've said to people—and we have, to a whole generation—that you live in a world that can end at any moment," then you make "the end of the world" a conscious possibility.

The Bible, too, talks about the end of the world, he concedes. But what is different today is the recognition that the end "need not come from some supernatural source. There are people now living who can push the buttons . . . and start that chain reaction that can do it.

"When we ask people to live with that idea, it affects their sense of responsibility." One result: By putting "man in the position of the supernatural," he says, you logically raise the question "What do you need Him [God] for anymore?"

"I think the question one should ask is: Will religion disappear?" He doesn't believe it will. "I think that what is challenged is *current modes* of religion, not religion. There's so much about man himself that is still a mystery to man, no matter how much we discover."

Richards also notes that the change in humanity's

"sense of responsibility" has ramifications for our attitudes toward the earth.

"If you read, as I read a few weeks ago, that we now believe that we can depart this planet and set up existence elsewhere—what a fabulous thing that is," says Richards. But, he adds, "what a tremendous and horrific thing that is, because it relieves us of a certain responsibility. If we do succeed in destroying the earth, there are some of us who need not be destroyed with it—and who can depart, observe it from afar, and start something else someplace else.

"A couple of years ago we were worried about destroying the earth—which meant destroying ourselves and the future. And that responsibility for the future—that big thing that weighs on us all, which is our responsibility to future generations—that was an aspect of our concern about the destruction of the earth.

"But now," he says, his actor's voice slipping into tones of muted irony, "we can even be relieved from *that*. We can go someplace else. The earth can be discarded like any other product—disposable rubbish."

After all, "we now create a lot of rubbish—and some of it we can't even destroy any longer."

As with our consumer products, he suggests, so with the earth. "We are a rubbish-creating society, and we can make rubbish out of the earth. What does it all mean?"

That last question—"What does it all mean?"—brings Richards squarely into the domain of the arts.

"The arts must in some way retain a position of attempting to find perspective for man in all of this." They must, he explains, "define whatever the new society is that we're evolving—to find what are the values, and, I hope, to try to find better methods of human exchange and interchange."

So while the role of the arts may not be "going through something that is new, historically," he says it is "going through something that is new and tremendous to those of us who are living it, because our world is at stake."

And it is precisely because the arts are willing to explore the pivotal questions of the age—up to and including the survival of the species—that Richards thinks they will play a central role in the 21st century.

If, that is, we don't put too many constraints on the artists. "Art is created with one basic limitation, and that's the imagination of the artist." But society sets up other boundaries as well. "We put boundaries of time," he explains. "We say, 'If you're going to create this piece, you've got so many hours within so many weeks to do it.' We say, 'You've got so much money,' which means that you've got a limitation of personnel and rehearsal time. And you've got a limitation on the artists you can engage.

"At what point is it no longer art? I think we will have to address that."

What about the threats to the arts from the entertainment media? Will humanity in the 21st century seek amusement rather than enlightenment?

By way of an answer, he turns to a discussion of television. "The reason that I think that the theater can survive television is because of perspective."

He acknowledges that "all of the startling events of our time will happen on television." Because of television, he says, "we've already seen war, which used to be a mythic thing that people did someplace else. . . . We've seen assassinations, we've seen murder, we've seen the starving—whatever the monumental events of our time are, we've been there, we've seen them."

He also acknowledges that, in the portrayal of events,

television is an invaluable tool. Through television, he says, "I can instantly be in Reykjavik, right outside the door, waiting to see up close the look on the face of my president. . . . I can make my assessment of just what has happened. I didn't get through the door, but I can be the first to see.

"Television has that power. It isn't just the words. Now, as we both look, the reporter and I, at that face, I can have a different interpretation. Without the ability to look at that face, I'm stuck with the reporter's interpretation."

But that very power, for Richards, raises a grave concern about television. "At what point do we become inured," he asks, to the problems around us? As he sees television coverage of starving children first in one place and then in another, Richards worries about the "danger of a reduced effect."

"Just how are we responding as human beings to being placed in all of these events as they're happening? We certainly have to be conscious of television as a very potent force, and its use has to be understood. . . . We have to be very careful and very smart to deal with it."

One of the dangers he sees in the future, in fact, lies in television's ability to create celebrities. Richards contrasts the little-known actor doing excellent work in a regional theater with "someone who has a running part on a soap opera and who is an immediate celebrity and can't get through the supermarket.

"Celebrity has very little to do with the quality of . . . artistry." Yet it is a subject that "the future has to address" if the best artists are going to be "respected and supported."

At bottom, however, Richards distinguishes between *seeing* the events and *understanding* them—which, for him, is a way of distinguishing television from theater. The former, he suggests, is an attempt to represent reality. He describes the latter, however, as "a manipulation of reality, a provocation through reality to fantasy, intended to provoke, to make you think, or to persuade or to exercise you in some way."

And that provocation, for Richards, requires the live interaction that only theater can provide. "I think that nothing that can be devised—and maybe I'm going way out on a limb to say this—can displace or replace human interaction."

That's why "a theater is an exciting place to be. It is also a dangerous place to be, because living people are there—there is communication that is going on in so many different ways. It isn't just from the stage to the audience, it's from each individual audience member to the stage and each individual member to each other.

"I don't think that we have devised anything to replace that kind of communication. I think as long as that exists, we will have theater. We will have people telling stories and . . . having conversations. And the theater is a conversation."

Andrei Voznesensky

Needing the Unexpectable

"Why do you write poems?" Andrei Voznesensky was asked at a recent reading.

"By instinct," he replied. "Why do you live?"

That instinct has brought Voznesensky, one of the Soviet Union's foremost poets, to prominence at home as well as abroad, where his works have been translated into English and most other Western European languages.

While he was still a schoolboy, that instinct also led him to send some poems to Boris Pasternak. The result was a close friendship over many years and a strong attachment to Pasternak's anti-Stalinist values.

"Pasternak told me, 'Don't go to Institute of Literature, because they will only kill you,' " he recalls.

He enrolled instead at the Architectural Institute in Moscow. When he began publishing poems in 1958 during the Soviet Union's ten-year cultural "thaw," he became immensely popular, along with Yevgeny Yevtushenko, as a voice of poetic protest. After 1963, when Nikita Khrushchev criticized him severely, Voznesensky spent years without being published. In 1978, however, he won the State Prize for Poetry for his volume Stained-Glass Craftsman.

"Voznesensky always worked within the system," says Tufts University Russian professor David Sloan, "criticizing in-

equities where he found them, but not becoming a dissident." Voz-
nesensky has championed the first publication inside the Soviet
Union of Vladimir Nabokov's works and of Pasternak's Doctor
Zhivago, and is dedicated to organizing exhibitions inside the
Soviet Union of Marc Chagall's paintings. A strong supporter of
Russian rock music, he has written the libretto for a rock opera, Juno
and Perchance.

Cambridge, Massachusetts

Over early-morning tea in a motel coffee shop Andrei
Voznesensky hardly looks like one of the foremost Soviet
poets. Trim, clean shaven, dressed in a tweed jacket and a silk
scarf, he could easily pass for a professor or an international
businessman.

But his message carries the same protest that once
caused Soviet leader Nikita Khrushchev, in a towering rage,
to order him to "clear out of my country." It is a message
that more recently brought fourteen thousand people together in a Moscow sports stadium to hear him read. During
a month-long tour through the United States to promote his
latest collection of poems, *An Arrow in the Wall*, it has been a
message that has left audiences energized, moved, and de-
lighted.

Now, in soft-spoken English charged with Slavic vow-
els, he turns his attention to the 21st century.

"We need a revolution of the mind," he says simply.

He builds to that point by commenting on two
significant characteristics of modern society. The first, he
notes, is "very banal: Everybody has said it." It is the need
for international agreements to control weapons—nuclear as
well as conventional.

"Nobody wants war," he adds, except possibly "some
adventurous, crazy generals." What worries him is a war that
might arise "by chance."

"Our country doesn't trust you," he says, "and your country doesn't trust us." That, he adds, "can be dangerous not only for you and us but for everybody." He worries in particular about "what happens in your lab or our lab" as weapons research moves into genetic technology.

How can the threat be stemmed? "We have to open our labs" for international inspection.

A second characteristic of modern life, Voznesensky notes, is the increasing interrelatedness of nations. Nowadays, he says, "we have no borders—and this is both good and bad." He values every evidence of a breakdown of political borders: His current trip to the United States ("I was not sent," he insists) came after only two weeks' wait for permission from the Soviet authorities. But he also points to some problems. "Chernobyl had no borders," he notes, referring to the radiation that spread into Europe following the explosion at a Soviet nuclear power plant in 1986. "Acid rain has no borders."

"There are borders geographical and borders of the mind. But people now don't understand this, and they stay very primitive—thinking about ego inside borders."

The challenge for the 21st century is to "stop the ego"—the self-absorption that occurs "not only in a personal sense, but in a national sense." The need will be to "think about our neighbor, about other persons and cultures.

"That is why we need first a new way of thinking, a new vocabulary." Today "we have 19th-century thinking. But technology is so fast—everything is traveling so fast. Everything is speeding more than our brains, so we have to change our brains to make our mentality 21st-century. If we don't, we will die."

Warmaking is "19th-century thinking," the result of one nation's desire to impose its ego on another. Also "19th-century" is the desire of ruling powers "to take some countries by occupation"—a desire he perceives in the Soviet invasion of Afghanistan. Grilled about Afghanistan during his poetry reading at Tufts University the evening prior to the interview, Voznesensky replied, "I am against this war," and said that it had been begun under then Soviet leader Leonid Brezhnev and that it would not last.

The need to reach beyond such "19th-century thinking," in fact, underlies Voznesensky's work as a poet.

"That is why I'm so for art—not realistic art, but very modern art, experimental art, because this art will give us a new kind of thinking.

"When you see classics like [the paintings of] Salvador Dali, or Picasso, or my friend Robert Rauschenberg, you perhaps cannot agree with them, but immediately they give you another possible way to look at the world.

"That is why I am fighting in Russia for modern art: not because I am an artist but because these modern paintings and literature show people how to think about economics, politics, and agriculture."

Experiencing such art, he says, people "will think something new. They will do the same as Salvador Dali, but in economics. Otherwise we die. We need something unexpected."

"I think the future will be in cooperating." He adds that the goal must be to draw the best elements from both East and West.

"We have terrible sides in our country, terrible," he says, referring to the Soviet Union. But, while noting that "I love your country," he says there are "some things I don't like" about the United States.

"Somebody asked me, 'Would you like to have an American economy?' I said, 'Yes, in many respects.' But we must not lose this interest in art, in literature." What he likes least about the U.S., he says, is that "literature, art, is not so important here."

The contrast with the Soviet Union, in fact, is striking. At home, Voznesensky enjoys a popularity usually accorded only to Western film stars. A speech he made recently in Moscow, protesting plans for an ill-conceived public monument, sparked such a popular outcry that the government reversed direction. Since then, his telephone has been ringing constantly with calls for help.

"I'm not a powerful man. I have no high job, I have no motor car with a special telephone. But as a poet, if I ask an [official in] high authority—if I call and ask, 'Please, look, we need something'—in Russia, they love poetry. For them, poetry is something special. If I ask, they do it, because they want to do something for a poet."

Not surprisingly, the great danger Voznesensky sees facing both superpowers in the 21st century is the undercutting of artistic expression by what he calls "standardization."

"Certainly I'm afraid of [the increasing number] of weapons," he says, "but I'm more afraid of raising people to be standard—to make robots from people."

In particular, he worries about what he calls "the losing of personality, individuality." In the Soviet Union, "where you cannot stand all this blah-blah-blah-blah-blah standard" of rhetoric, people tend to become indifferent and apathetic.

"But in your country," he says, "people become standard, too." He sees a danger of a loss of individuality in a society where moneymaking, competition, and what he calls "fighting" are so important.

"I'm not interested in the 21st century if it will be only robots. It can happen, but it will be death: We will be alive, but dead. And that is why I'm very eager about our art, about poetry. We need it like vitamins."

What qualities would he draw from East and West to fashion a way of thinking for the 21st century?

"You have the best economy," he says. "Maybe what we can learn from you is incentive." He faults the Soviet worker for being "lazy," for "smoking all day long" instead of working, and for drinking heavily. But he notes that free enterprise is making itself felt in the Soviet Union. "Now we have the first private restaurant, the first private taxi drivers." Gesturing across the table to include the now-bustling coffee shop, he notes that sooner or later "all the economy like this has to be private."

But Voznesensky has already found, if only anecdotally, an adverse side to American privatization. Because he composes his poems in his head while walking—"ten kilometers, at the end is my poem"—he needs space to walk.

"I wanted to write last week on the West Coast, near San Francisco," he recalls. Out for the day with a friend, he found himself inspired by a "very beautiful beach, a very beautiful place to write. But my friend said, 'No, you can't go there, because it is private.'

"She called the owner and said, 'Can you allow a Russian poet to go to your beach to have inspiration?' and he said, 'Certainly, go!' But it was too long preparation, and my inspiration stopped.

"For me," Voznesensky concludes, "it is strange and not nice when this forest you can't enjoy, this piece of sea belongs to somebody."

For Voznesensky, the great Russian contribution to the 21st century will be in matters of the human spirit.

"Maybe the brain of your nation is better," he concedes. But "our instinct is better, yes?"

"From us the main thing [that the 21st century can learn] is spiritual things, like literature." He notes that in the Soviet Union "religion was stopped" after the revolution, at least officially. But the spiritual needs remained. Now, he says, "poetry is like a new religion: It's something very spiritual."

Is he, then, an optimist? The question has a sobering effect. Leaning forward, Voznesensky answers with a guarded melancholy. "I try to make something to make me optimistic," he says cryptically. "Working and trying— because even in this bad situation you have to find a way."

Then is he worried that Soviet leader Mikhail Gorbachev's policy of *glasnost* (openness) will not survive into the immediate future—not to mention the 21st century?

"In my heart, I don't think about this. I try to work hard, and I'm sure that if I work hard it will be more reason that *glasnost* will be not stopped. Because I know there is terrible resistance" inside the Soviet Union to these reforms. "Now it is a fight like war. I hope that we'll win. I hope. Gorbachev has said that he wants this process not to stop. But we have to stop this wind resistance."

Down through Russian history, he explains, "if the czar or our leader wants to replace officials with new people, what did he do? He asked the police and army to arrest the people and kill them. But now Gorbachev, for the first time in our history, wants to make revolution by a democratic way. It's very difficult. But it's fantastic, because he really wants to make it by democracy, not arresting people. But it is dangerous—because he uses this method, but [his opponents] do not. They are people of very dishonest methods."

Before the trip which included his reading at Tufts, Voznesensky refused invitations to read his poetry in Spain, Italy, India, and other nations. Had he been able to, he would also have postponed his American trip. "I wanted to stay in Russia, to help this process. If more people did this, things would be better. We have many active enemies, and we have many indifferent people who are afraid what will be tomorrow."

Throughout his conversation, however, one element of his faith burns brightly: his trust in the youth. "We have to think of youth," he says. "They are not yet very wise, but by instinct they are making what is for the next century."

He describes an art exhibition held in Moscow several months before he left for America—the first of its kind in which "they gave the gallery to only youngsters without any control." Daily there were "a thousand people waiting at the door," and in the evenings they held rock concerts.

"The atmosphere was good, everything was great," he recalls. But among those who presented their work was "not yet one genius."

"We need time," he says—time to develop the talent of the youth, time for "books to be written.

"They are not smart, but they feel by instinct, by blood, that they have something new, a new morality that is pure."

Carlos Fuentes

The Gruyère Cheese of Progress

"I see the world verbally," says Mexican novelist-diplomat Carlos Fuentes. "You say truth, you say justice, you say democracy, you say development—words don't create them, but if they do not exist in words they will never exist."

Born in Panama, Fuentes spent his early years in Santiago, Chile; Rio de Janeiro; Montevideo, Uruguay; Buenos Aires; Quito, Ecuador; and Washington, as his father, a Mexican diplomat, changed posts. "I started writing when I was seven years old," he recalls, describing a newspaper written in crayon, which he tried to circulate through his Washington apartment building.

Three years later his political consciousness surfaced in the RKO Keith movie theater in Washington when, during a film about Sam Houston, he shouted, "Viva Mexico! Death to the Gringos!" His father dragged him from the theater—and then proudly leaked the story to the Washington Star.

After studying law in Mexico City and holding various posts in the Ministry of Foreign Affairs, Fuentes published his first novel, Where the Air Is Clear, *in 1958—a book recognized as launching "El Boom" in Latin American fiction. In 1962 he published his best-known work,* The Death of Artemio Cruz, *followed in 1976 by* Terra Nostra *and, more recently, by* The Old Gringo.

Fuentes, who served as Mexico's ambassador to France from

1975 to 1977, insists that in Latin America writers must become politically involved. An outspoken critic of United States foreign policy in Latin America, he has in the past been denied entry to the United States under the McCarran-Walter Act. He now divides his time between Mexico and various university appointments in Europe and the United States.

London

Carlos Fuentes is an optimist. That much comes through in his vigorous tone of voice, in his animated gestures, in his love of humanity—and even in the relish with which he approaches an elegant English breakfast at a London hotel.

But he is an optimist standing on a precipice. Ahead of him, stretching into the 21st century, lie two great fears with which, he says, humanity must come to terms. The first is fear of nuclear annihilation. The second is fear that the developing nations will either be crushed out or swallowed up by the developed world.

And behind him, where he turns for explanations of how the world came to its present state, lies the wreckage of what he calls "the philosophies that have guided the Western world at least since the 18th century."

What characterizes those philosophies is "the basic belief in happiness—that happiness is attainable on earth, that humanity and its institutions are infinitely perfectible.

"I think this is what has come crumbling down," Fuentes says. "In the midst of the greatest material progress, of the greatest technical progress ever achieved, we have seen all its limitations."

This particular view, he says with a ready smile, is "the response of all those who see the big holes in the Gruyère cheese of progress."

Fuentes notes that the past several centuries have seen "a great addiction to materialism" and an unthinking willingness to define progress in material terms. "This is what has failed."

"The *material* rewards of progress are as nothing compared to what are supposed to be the *moral* rewards of progress. I am not against material progress. I am against the consciousness that material progress will solve our problems."

What are those problems? The foremost is the fear that a "nuclear winter" could engulf a planet "devoured by catastrophe." Throughout history, "we've always known that man and woman can destroy themselves. But we have always known, throughout the ages, that nature would remain while we disappeared . . . if only to bear witness to our folly and our pride.

"Today, I think for the first time in history, we have the consciousness that nature can disappear along with us," he says, adding that "it really shakes your soul." The Greek playwright Sophocles, for all his tragic vision, "could not imagine this," but nowadays "we can."

"It unites us as human beings through fear as we have never been united before."

That very unity, he feels, "is one of the great strengths of the approaching century. So many barriers that used to keep us apart now have disappeared, and we are more and more united."

That unity, however, is "a condition born of fear. I hope that in the 21st century it will be transformed into a condition made of hope."

The second problem on Fuentes's agenda concerns what he describes as "the enormous gap" between the political, economic, social, and technological conditions of industrial nations and those of developing nations. As a result, he says, the developing nations in the 21st century will face a clash between what he calls "the project of independence"— their ongoing efforts to shed what was once a colonial status—and "the project of interdependence" that increasingly makes the world's nations reliant on one another.

"We have this socioeconomic or political fear that our national projects will be swallowed up by transnational companies," he explains, "and that we will have little say in our own destiny.

"No matter how far we have gone in certain cases, the developing world has been totally outstripped by the incredible development of modern technology and concentration of power on the international scene."

It is this concentration of power in the hands of the two superpowers that Fuentes sees as particularly damaging to the developing nations. In the 21st century, he hopes to see "the disintegration of bipolar politics as the dominating factor" in world affairs. He hopes for "a multipolar politics in which there are many centers of power."

For that reason Fuentes is particularly eager to see an end to the arms race. "Without the arms race, the United States is much less of a power—and the Soviet Union is no power at all."

Fuentes, who expresses an ardent belief in democracy and his great affection for the United States, acknowledges that the end of the arms race would leave each superpower facing "an incredible conundrum."

"The conundrum" for the Soviet Union centers upon the fact that its armaments alone confer upon it "a big-power status"—since it lacks the "technologies of information and the access to them by the people" that could make it a genuinely "modern society."

That being the case, says Fuentes, the present arms race simply has the effect of "furthering the anachronism of the Soviet Union" in its efforts to "be a strong society merely on military terms."

Fuentes sees a very different conundrum facing the

United States—also related to the arms race and to the baffling (from a developing-nations perspective) foreign policy that results from it.

"Can the United States," he asks, "go on forever being a democracy inside and an empire abroad? Can it keep this juggling act up for long?"

Fuentes worries that, if this conundrum persists much longer, it will create "a pattern in which eventually it will be impossible for the internal democracy to respond to the external empire."

"My great hope as a friend of the United States" is that "the democracy will coincide inside and out. And then the power of the United States in the Western hemisphere will be such as it has never imagined."

Driving the U.S. toward what Fuentes calls its "empire abroad" is its concern over communism, especially in Central America. That problem, for Fuentes, does not represent a significant threat to the 21st century.

"There is no communist threat in Central America." In the first place, the history of the countries there makes a communist form of government "culturally impossible," given "the extremely strong Catholic component" in the politics and culture of the region. For example, Fuentes notes that "the whole concept of St. Thomas's [Thomas Aquinas's] politics of the common good is finally the center of politics in Nicaragua"—and is a far cry from the materialism of communism.

In the second place, he says, the Soviet Union cannot logistically sustain an operation in Nicaragua, given the long distance between the two countries and the state of the Soviet economy.

Even Cuba, where such an operation has been sustained, does not represent in Fuentes's mind a long-term problem: He predicts, before the end of the 21st century, some kind of "arrangement with Cuba" that brings it back into much closer contact with the United States.

But the heart of Fuentes's concerns about the United States' relationship to the developing world seems to have less to do with politics than with culture. What intrigues him about a "multipolar" world in which the superpowers were less dominant is that it would also be "a multiracial world and a multicultural world."

"If there is not the understanding that cultures are different, and that people have different ways of responding to the basic realities of life and economics and politics and love and eating and a million things because of what their cultures have been, then we can't understand each other."

The U.S., he says, "may think that the solution for the United States, the culture of the United States, is the universal culture and should benefit everyone. Well, no! No! I will not change a wonderful *mole* from Oaxaca [in Mexico] for a hamburger. I will not. And my politics will respond to the *mole*.

"This has to be understood by the United States, which has a democratic culture," he insists. "I don't expect Moscow to understand that the Czechs have their own culture."

For Fuentes, the culture of a nation resides not in its institutions but in its people—in what he calls its "society." The problem of the developing world, he says, has been the failure of institutions to come to grips with the ills facing society—especially in Latin America. That has led, in his view, to oppressive forms of government and a "history of unpunished violence" in the region.

The result for the next century could be "a big, big struggle between the democratic tendencies and the authoritarian tendencies." But it could also be a time of promise. "I hope now that we can enter the 21st century in Latin America with an agenda in which [the three main institutions of] church, army, and state are finally less important than the society.

"During the 20th century we searched for a state that would control the church and the army"—a search that, in his view, failed. "I hope we can enter the 21st century with a society that can control the church, the army, and the state as well. It's called democracy—not perhaps Anglo-Saxon democracy, but some extension of Thomistic democracy" as in St. Thomas's "politics of the common good."

"We have to find our own Hispanic democratic solution," he says, adding, "what we cannot accept is the United States imposing its political solutions, its brand of democracy."

On two other points, too, Fuentes hopes for progress. One is population control, which he finds especially important in his own land. "I don't think there can be a really developing society—one that takes into account the village life, the life of the majority of the Mexican people—without some kind of family planning."

Another is the environment. He faults developing-nation policies for much of the degradation, citing a willingness of some governments to overlook industrial pollution in order to attract lucrative investments from abroad.

He sees a remedy in more democratization of the developing world under the direction not of "state" but of "society."

Why, in Fuentes's view, does the United States—whose democracy he so clearly admires—seem so bent on "imposing" its own solutions to the problems in the developing world?

"We tend to think in Latin America that we have memory and you have the media, and that's the big difference.

"The role of Latin America is to make the United States understand that memory counts—that there is history, and that it does not renew itself every twenty-four hours when Dan Rather appears on the set and defines the history of the day, which will be renewed the next day so that the memory of the previous day can be thrown into the garbage can."

For Fuentes the novelist, the artist has a crucial role to play in providing a proper sense of this "memory."

"High on the agenda for the 21st century will be the need to restore some kind of tragic consciousness." Needed, he says, is a view of the world reflected in "the most ancient wisdom of the West": that "progress does not assure happiness" and the world is "not divided into good guys and bad guys."

"The world is made of grace," Fuentes says, "and the important thing is to understand that . . . we are all struggling between values."

"Could we restore a perspective," he asks, "in which values are in conflict, and not good and evil—which is simply melodrama?"

Admirable Models

VI

The absence of admirable models has an effect on all of this—
and the examples of the *unadmirable* being the success stories.

—Barbara Tuchman

Olusegun Obasanjo

Jimmy Carter

Richard von Weizsäcker

Olusegun Obasanjo

Waking the Slumbering Giant

The previous sections have sketched in the future according to philosophers, historians, economists, scientists, and artists. Each has articulated—sometimes overtly, sometimes implicitly—a view of the world as it must be if it is to survive the next century. And each has put stern demands on the institutions of government—particularly on the statesmen and politicians who, as heads of state, will help guide the world into its third millennium.

The three individuals in this final section—Olusegun Obasanjo, Jimmy Carter, and Richard von Weizsäcker—speak from the experience of national leadership and international responsibility. They have come from different backgrounds and specialities. But their careers have molded them into generalists. To make sense of our multifaceted world, they have had to comprehend the principles of economics, technology, history, and a dozen other disciplines. As statesmen, however, they have had to do more. Being practitioners of politics—defined by the eminent historian H. A. L. Fisher as "the art of human happiness"—they have been charged with turning the vision into the practicality, the theory into the law, and the desirable into the possible. Having lived daily with the future, they are particularly suited to conclude this series of interviews.

The first voice is that of General Olusegun Obasanjo, Nigeria's former head of state. "I call myself a chicken farmer," he says with a broad laugh. "Some of my friends don't like that, but some do!" His farming, however, is no laughing matter. After turning over the reins of his military government to civilian rule in 1979, General Obasanjo turned to agriculture with uncommon zeal: He now keeps some 200,000 layers and 400,000 broilers on his acreage near the city of Abeokuta, Nigeria.

"I was born and bred on a farm," he says, noting that Nigeria, whose economy has been severely jolted by the fall in oil prices, needs to return to the agricultural self-sufficiency it enjoyed before independence.

Obasanjo was educated at Abeokuta Baptist High School and at Mons Officer Cadet School in Britain. After joining the Nigerian Army in 1958, he served in the Congo (now Zaire) in 1960, later commanding a commando division during the Nigerian civil war. As head of state he was credited with helping to promote discipline and moderation in Nigerian society.

Since stepping down from that position, he has been increasingly involved in international affairs. With former Australian Prime Minister Malcolm Fraser, he co-chaired the Commonwealth mission to South Africa (known as the Eminent Persons Group), which visited South Africa in 1986 and made recommendations to the forty-nine-member Commonwealth. A staunch supporter of the United Nations, he is often mentioned as a possible future secretary-general.

New York

Leaning back from the dining-room table, General Olusegun Obasanjo drops his already soft, British-accented voice still lower.

"What really *is* security?" he muses. "Can we be secure when our adversaries are insecure? Shouldn't we now be considering security in terms of what we call *common* security—which makes you secure because your seeming adversary feels secure?

"You cannot talk of peace without security. If you feel threatened, you are not going to really feel in harmony with your neighbor."

As he speaks, the midmorning sunlight filters into a colleague's elegant Upper East Side apartment, where Obasanjo stays on his frequent visits to New York. This morning, the man who in 1970 accepted the surrender of the Biafran forces in Nigeria's civil war is expanding on the importance of security for the 21st century.

It must be a security based not on military force, he says, but on disarmament.

"We definitely have to address the issue of disarmament in all its ramifications: nuclear weapons, conventional weapons, chemical weapons," he says.

"This is an issue that, if we do not resolve it, will consume us."

Some people ask, he says, why citizens of African nations should worry about nuclear disarmament.

"It does not matter in which part of the world we live, it does not matter in what condition we live in the world," he tells them. "The issue of disarmament affects each and every one of us.

"I believe that there are some things that we do not even know about the total effect of a world caught in a nuclear conflagration." From what we do know, he says, in such a situation "no amount of medical services would be able to cope with the wounded, not to talk of the dead."

Equally pressing, however, is the effect of armaments on a world *not* at war. "The stockpiles of weapons—be they nuclear, chemical, or conventional—have a destabilizing effect for the security of the world. And they have grave implications for our ability to address the serious economic situation of the revitalization of the world economy and of sustainable growth, of cooperation and development."

Olusegun Obasanjo   *169*

He feels there are "more than adequate" resources in the world. "It's just a question of distributing them fairly, reducing waste, reducing excessive consumption.

"I'm not talking only in terms of international situations of North [the industrial nations] and South [the developing nations], as they are now called, but also in terms of the *national* North-and-South divide," he adds, explaining that "just as you have the North-and-South divide within the world, within each nation you have a certain amount of North and South.

"And in almost every nation, the resources that have been diverted to armament . . . could easily be diverted to reducing or eliminating the North-South divide—and of course the greater North-South divide internationally."

The issue, for Obasanjo, reaches beyond nuclear armament. Just as important is the reduction of conventional weapons. That issue, he says, has particularly important implications "within developing countries."

"Since the end of World War II, more than one hundred and sixty wars have been waged in different parts of the developing world. We have lost more lives and properties in these wars than were lost in World War II."

If such "senseless waste" has not commanded the same kind of attention as nuclear disarmament, he says, that is only because these wars were thought of as "far away in developing countries."

Disarmament, then, is "an issue that world leaders must address," because "it concerns all of them." Needed, he says, is "a new conception and a new idea of security—not in terms of how much we can outgun and outstockpile weapons against ourselves, but how much we can cooperate, how much we can understand ourselves, how much we can work together."

How can such cooperation be achieved? The answer lies in what Obasanjo calls "communication."

"In spite of the technological development in the field of communication," he notes, "we are still not communicating enough—especially the political leadership. It is sad commentary on how much we have *not* developed human instinct beyond the base level of many centuries back.

"For five years the leaders of the two superpowers completely cut off communication at the political level between themselves. Yet we can talk to people on the moon— we can talk to any place in the world today instantaneously.

"I think this is one thing that has to improve. The facilities are there, the technology has been provided. It's just a question of us using the technology to communicate, to understand ourselves through communication, and to be able to put ourselves across to ourselves in a way that we will be able to cooperate and reduce threat and fear.

"I don't believe that any human being is absolutely and completely evil. There must be some good in him. Why don't we, through communication, find out what are the other man's fears, hopes, aspirations?

"We will not know about ourselves only through spies and satellites. We will know more about ourselves through communications."

Along with the disarmament-communication issue, the other major topic on Obasanjo's agenda is something he describes as "three in one": environmental protection, population control, and the redistribution of resources.

He says the problem of the environment is "almost as bad as the problem of disarmament, because it knows no national frontier or regional limit. It will encompass all of us, it will affect all of us. And in the end, we may all be destroyed piecemeal by it.

"Again, it is an issue that requires concerted effort of political leaders all over the world. I believe that God or the Maker of the world, as a great artist, created the world with an adequate balance of what is required for us to enjoy this world—and that human beings [have begun to] disrupt the balance. The implications for us in the coming century are very serious, maybe disastrous."

Here again, he notes, "there is sufficient resource availability to be able to redress adequately the degradation of the environment." The problem, however, is "tied up inextricably" with the problem of population growth.

"I'm not saying that the population of the world now is too much for the world. There are, of course, areas where the population is slightly heavier than other places. But as I said, the resources of earth are adequate—if only we are able to ensure some form of redistribution."

Nevertheless, he insists, population-control measures are essential. The problem is that "where population is rising fastest is where people are the poorest."

It's like self-destruction. Unless you have a way that population is put under control, whatever else you want to do—redistribution of resources and all that—will just not make any impact.

"I believe it can be done. Population control has of course happened in the developed world."

"The economic factor," he says, is a "major factor of bringing about population control"—noting, as many demographers have, the correlation between rising economic prosperity and falling birthrates. But Obasanjo insists that economic improvement must go hand in hand with education.

"Where the education is there, the economic factor helps," he says. But where there is no development of education, he warns, efforts to improve economic prosperity will not in themselves have the desired effect.

What, then, of Africa's role in the 21st century?

The danger, as Obasanjo sees it, is of the rest of the world ignoring Africa—and of Africa's "going the way it's going" at present.

At the time of independence from colonial rule, he recalls, both Africans and outsiders had "great expectations" that the new nations would be able to "manage their own affairs."

"The expectations were unrealized on both sides," he recalls. "Africans had their hopes dashed—partly through the fault of their own leadership, and partly through the fault of the world in which they lived."

In addition, outsiders who expected a "new giant" to rise from his "slumber" saw, instead, "this giant really sleeping and not waking up. And then, of course, they said, 'Well, look, we might as well leave this giant there to continue its slumber.' "

The result is that "Africa continues to be seen as the continent of drought, famine, civil wars—a place that can be ignored and that in fact substantially has been ignored."

But "if peace is indivisible," says Obasanjo, then "for as long as Africa continues to be ignored, in fact that may be the tension, the major area of conflict in the 21st century."

In such circumstances, he says, there could be an increase of conflicting interests in Africa by the developed world—particularly the United States, the Soviet Union, and Europe. "And then you have the possibility of real, serious catastrophe—in terms of human suffering, in terms of violent conflict, in terms of a retrogression in development."

These things, however, "are factors that can be reversed if the world can collectively take care of resource distribution, population control, and control of the environment.

"If Africa becomes a positive contributor to peace, security, economic cooperation, and economic development in the world," then "that part of the world will to a large extent cease to be a destabilizing factor in the equation of international peace and security."

Improvements in African living standards "will have implications for America, Europe, the socialist bloc, and the third world as a whole. With more position and power, Africa can then contribute more meaningfully, more actively, and more positively to the economic progress of the world through world trade."

The result, he predicts, will be "more cohesion in Africa itself." A continent that currently has "fifty-four countries or thereabouts" will, in the 21st century, "probably consolidate to not more than five or six countries that can really be able to do the planning, the working, and the effective implementation of Africa's development and its cooperation with the rest of the world."

That will require, he says, "serious rethinking of the boundaries that we inherited from the colonial powers." Asked whether history provides any examples of such consolidation among nations, he points to the European Community—and to the early history of the United States. He concedes that such a consolidation will not be easy. But he adds, "I have no doubt in my mind that we will have to address this issue at one time or another—in the next century, if not in this."

But wouldn't tribal ties and nationalistic feelings interfere with such changes?

"When you talk of the tribalism," he says, "that hasn't worried me much. Over the past twenty-five years there have been internal conflicts in Africa. But no country has really broken into two. In spite of conflicts, they all realize, at the end of the day, the value of living together."

He predicts a movement in Africa away from what he calls the "politics of ethnicity" to the "politics of nationalism . . . and resource creation."

Ultimately, he says, "we will see that we have to coalesce, we have to come together."

Jimmy Carter

Meaningful Alternatives

When the four buff-colored pavilions of the Carter Presidential Center in Atlanta opened to the public in the fall of 1986, former United States President Jimmy Carter noted that "this is one time that the dream was exceeded by the reality."

His "dream," as Carter has said, is to "gather thoughtful people from all walks of life" to pursue "meaningful alternatives to even the most controversial and intransigent problems." With that in mind, Carter has devoted much of his energy since leaving the White House in 1981 to the establishment of the center. In addition to housing some 27 million documents from his presidency, the facility provides a home for a new public-policy think tank (the Carter Center of Emory University), as well as for the Carter-Menil Human Rights Foundation and for Global 2000 Inc., which studies worldwide problems of hunger, health, and the environment.

James Earl Carter, born in Plains, Georgia, graduated from the United States Naval Academy in 1946 and worked in the Navy's nuclear submarine program. In 1953 he returned to the family farm in Georgia, operated a profitable seed and farm-supply business, and was a deacon and Sunday-school teacher in his local church. Elected to the Georgia Senate in 1962, he became governor of Georgia in 1971. In 1976, after winning a first-ballot nomination for president at the Democratic National Convention, he

was elected thirty-ninth president of the United States. He and his
wife, Rosalynn, now live in Plains.

Atlanta

"I think the greatest problem that we face is the relationship between the advanced nations and the poverty-stricken nations."

For Jimmy Carter, that crisply phrased point dominates the agenda for the next century. It runs like a thread through the public displays here at the newly opened Carter Presidential Center. It shapes the work of the several Carter-sponsored public policy organizations housed within the center's four circular pavilions. And it echoes throughout a half-hour interview in Carter's sunny, modern office overlooking the twin manmade ponds of the center's Japanese garden.

Between the nations of the industrial North and the developing South, Carter says, "is a chasm that hasn't, so far, been bridged."

Nor, among the leaders of what he calls the "rich nations," is there "an adequate awareness" of the problems facing the poorer nations.

The problems he enumerates include environmental degradation, overpopulation, and international debt. They show up in the developing world as hunger, disease, poverty, and political instability. To Carter, they appear to be getting increasingly urgent.

Why this lack of awareness of developing-world problems? One reason, he says, is that the leadership of the industrial nations is split between "environmentalists, so-called, on the one hand, and the business and financial leaders on the other."

"This is another chasm that is rarely bridged." The

---

term *environmentalist* is, in the business community, "almost an expletive."

Yet "there are many environmentalists who, while they are quite enlightened and quite level-headed and responsible, look on the business community as surfeited with selfishness.

"I think that an inevitable relationship is going to develop between these two sides, either through enlightened planning or through the reaction to crises."

Carter notes that when he was elected president, "I was an avowed environmentalist. I was one of the founders of the major conservation organization in Georgia. But I faced problems that I had never known about before: acid rain, Alaska lands, polar regions, world population explosion, things of that kind."

To help get a handle on such issues, he established "a multidepartmental commitment called Global 2000—just to look at what is going to happen to this world by the end of this century. It was not a doom prediction. It was an analysis of some of the problems that we might face."

He laments the fact that the global planning process "has now been abandoned by our own country"—because, he says, of "President Reagan's philosophical aversion to planning, which seems to be an intrusion in the private affairs of business."

Other nations, however, have continued the process. "Japan and West Germany, for instance, have superb commitments, funded jointly by the business and financial and government organizations, to continue to look to the future."

As a result, he says, those nations not only are more aware of conditions in the third world but are also more aware of what markets will be opening up in ten years.

Such planning helps them estimate "what products will

be demanded, which people will be natural distributors, what will be the raw materials available.

"They're taking this information, which we are ignoring for the time being, and building upon it an increasing competitive advantage over the United States in addressing world markets."

The results, in Carter's eyes, are already evident.

"When I left office less than six years ago, we were the greatest creditor nation on earth. Now the United States is the greatest debtor nation on earth, which is a very rapid change. And the adverse consequences of this change are unpredictable. I think they are going to be much worse than anyone presently thinks."

Another financial facet of a lack of global planning is evident in "the third-world debt problem"—which, he says, has "multiple causes."

"It's not as though the lenders and the borrowers all of a sudden lost their senses and made irresponsible loans," he says. Nor was it "just because there was a massive infusion of OPEC oil money that had to be placed somewhere.

"The present inability of those debtor nations to repay their debts" arises from "long-term trends in environmental quality: Forests are being decimated, scarce land areas are eroding, production of land is dropping, the population is increasing. And the countries just can't produce enough even to service their debts.

"There are probably fifty nations on the earth now that will never repay the principal on their debt and in which it takes a substantial proportion of their earnings just to *service* their debt."

In the developed nations, "We look upon this as an attack on the substantiality or profitability of our bank stock. But with those people it's life or death."

One of the results of that crunch, he says, is political instability. In the developing world "there is a massive movement to the cities coupled with an urbanization program, which means that the urban population gains tremendous political power resulting in very greatly reduced prices for grain. And the farmers then move to the cities because they can't make a profit, and they increase the urban population, and the farms are neglected." The result is an increasing spiral of economic imbalance.

"These people become frustrated," he explains, and "this in many cases leads to revolution or to violence."

It also weakens what Carter, still an outspoken proponent of human rights, calls "the competitive advantage" of democracy over other systems. "If a family with a starving child, or children, is faced with the question, 'Do you want bread, or freedom?' it's not inevitable that they will say, 'I prefer freedom.' "

He worries that in such circumstances "sometimes a totalitarian government can offer—at least on a temporary basis—a more efficient government with better distribution of food than a democracy."

Does he feel that the industrial nations are increasingly less insulated from the spillover of such problems?

"Yes," he replies, "but so far more Americans are asking, 'How much money do they owe our banks or our government?' rather than 'What caused the revolution in Nicaragua? Why are the Salvadorans still not endorsing the Duarte government? What are the root causes of starvation in the Sudan or in other sub-Saharan nations or in Ethiopia?' "

Needed, he says, is "a partnership or cooperative arrangement" with those nations, which asks, " 'What can we do jointly about this common problem?'

"Perhaps the next major crisis for our country is going to be caused by Mexico," he says—largely because, he explains, "we are wedded to Mexico in an unbreakable fashion. And I think there's an increasing awareness now—at least in the South and Southwestern states—that Mexico's problems are our problems."

Current efforts to resolve the problems are "almost entirely a reaction to crises." Needed, instead, are some institutions that allow longer-term examination of the problems—such as, he says, the Carter Center of Emory University, one of the organizations housed at the Presidential Center here.

"We're working on some of these problems—trying to teach people how to grow more food grain, trying to immunize children around the world against deadly diseases, or trying to have conferences here that involve leaders of third-world nations."

Recently, the organization held a conference of about thirty chief executive officers of major corporations and an equal number of environmental leaders.

Nationwide, however, he is concerned that "there's no mechanism by which we can revive the Global 2000 process or form an alliance between the business and professional and financial community, on the one hand, and environmentalists on the other." Nor, he laments, is there any sort of "cooperation of a blue-ribbon-commission character" between the United States and Mexico.

The task of developing such mechanisms, he says, is "what we face in the future—between now and the year 2000 and maybe later—that is of paramount importance."

One particular aspect of the North-South "chasm" that greatly concerns the former president is the growth of global population, which he characterizes as "extraordinary."

World population, now about 5 billion, is predicted to double sometime in the 21st century. "Of that extra 5 billion people, 90 percent will be in Asia, Africa, and Latin America."

The consequences will be "increased dissension, increased animosity, uncontrollable numbers of refugees, increased tendency toward revolution or violence." The population glut will also produce "an increasing degree of competitiveness among the industrialized nations"—a process that, he believes, is already being exemplified in the U.S. by the move to establish trade barriers.

But even this thrust toward trade protectionism, in Carter's mind, is linked to a need for better planning. Already, he says, U.S. exports face increased competition arising from the successes of the "long-range planning process" as practiced in Europe and Japan.

"A few of our corporations are large enough to do such planning on their own," he notes, citing IBM as an example. "But those are rare examples. There is no umbrella organization [in the U.S.] that can say, 'Let's use our tremendous computer capacity and our tremendous university capabilities and our scientific and research capabilities to look to the future and ask what the role of the United States is going to be, economically or politically or socially, in this world of tomorrow.'

"We're not doing that at all," he charges, noting that instead the U.S. is "fumbling around from one crisis to another without paying any attention to the future."

Does humanity's answer lie (as it does for several others interviewed for this book) in some form of world government structure?

"I don't really think so," Carter says. "I think when you try to have an international governing body, you arouse political problems of such magnitude that they overshadow the economic and social problems and environmental problems about which I'm speaking."

Injecting such political considerations, he adds, "just

exacerbates an already extremely complex and difficult subject."

One of the problems of such an international forum—exemplified, he says, by the United Nations—is that "the third-world nations and their representatives almost always numerically are in the majority. And they use this majority power as an irresponsible means by which to attack the developed nations of the world.

"I think if you could peel off the political shell where people are trying to make points back home by vituperation, and let the economists and scientists and business leaders who share common goals and a common geographical arena be the major participants—I think that would be the best entree I could think of into a resolution of this problem.

"I want to emphasize in closing that I don't look upon this all as an inevitable catastrophe or a premonition of doom.

"It's a matter of asking, 'What are the potential problems? What are the opportunities of a great nation to help alleviate problems and also to help our own competitive place in the world?'

"The thing that we need to do is to say to the developing world, 'We're all in the same boat: Your problems are really my problems.'"

Richard von Weizsäcker

Preserving Nature

"For my generation, what mattered was to build a healthy state from ruins, to secure freedom, and to increase prosperity," Richard von Weizsäcker, president of the Federal Republic of Germany, has said. "But we cannot expect eternal gratitude from the following generation for what we built up. The young people of today are asking quite different questions."

It is as an asker of questions—and a listener to answers—that von Weizsäcker has won broad respect as a forward-looking statesman, thinker, and head of state.

In his highly symbolic, politically neutral post described as "guardian of the Constitution," he has formal responsibility for representing West Germany in international relations and, if necessary, convening or dissolving parliament. He also has informal responsibility for advising, warning, encouraging, and mediating among his country's many political and social groups.

Born in Stuttgart, he studied law and history at Oxford, Grenoble, and Göttingen universities before serving in an infantry regiment during World War II. After taking his law degree, he worked in industry until 1966, when he took a position with the Christian Democratic Party.

In 1969 he was elected to parliament, rising to vice-president of the Bundestag, parliament's lower house, in 1979 before taking

___

up a three-year stint as mayor of Berlin in 1981. From 1969 until his election as president in 1984, he was a member of the governing council of the German Protestant Church.

Bonn

The president of West Germany, Richard von Weizsäcker, has dozens of things on his mind. But on his agenda for the 21st century there's only one central item: the preservation of nature, or, to use the word he prefers, creation. In the course of an hour-long conversation in the presidential residence at Villa Hammerschmidt, however, von Weizsäcker expands that single-item agenda to embrace a whole world of issues—North-South relations, population growth, nuclear armament, energy supplies, and more.

Nevertheless, as he tells his visitor in his Oxford-accented English, "it will remain easy throughout our whole conversation for me to prove that every possible item you're going to mention has to do with my primary concern—namely, to preserve nature."

Leaning forward on a sofa, he explains his point: "We have been brought up, and our ancestors even more, to understand that nature is serving mankind." But in the future, "we will have to realize, in our daily decisions and forms of behavior, that finally we are nothing but a little part in the history of nature. And either we learn to preserve nature—or, if you wish, to preserve creation—or we will not survive."

For von Weizsäcker, the word *environment* is inadequate. "It comes from the notion that there's one center, and that is *me*," he explains. That notion, he says, leads people to assume that the real reason for caring for the environment is simply to ensure that humanity can "move ahead the way it wants to move ahead."

"I don't think that's proper. I don't think that's a sufficient way of understanding what we really have to learn. We have to preserve nature for nature's own sake, not simply for the sake of mankind."

A committed Lutheran, von Weizsäcker traces man's attitude toward nature back to a misinterpretation of the Old Testament. "What we read in the Bible about man having dominion over the earth," he says, referring to the first chapter of Genesis, "may have been misunderstood." By suggesting that man has a right to dominate nature, this passage has been "a tremendously dangerous incentive for misunderstanding."

In man's relation with nature over the centuries he has "taken his share, more or less properly." Nowadays, however, "the unbelievable speed of progress in science and technology has come to a point where, without us realizing it quickly enough, we have started to take more than our share." That, he says, means that we not only have "the capability of destroying pretty much of the environment" but of "destroying ourselves" as well.

"In general," he says, speaking of man's relation to nature, "I think this is *the* most important question" on the next century's agenda.

Growing directly out of von Weizsäcker's concern for nature is his special interest in preserving the world's dwindling rain forests.

"Intellectually, it's easy to understand why their preservation is so important for everyone on earth. But existentially it's rather difficult to experience that as really true, because you don't live in Brazil and you don't live in Malaysia and Cameroon."

As he explained in a recent speech, tropical rain forests "play an irreplaceable role as a regulator of world climate, reservoir of water, as a natural cleaning filter for the atmo-

sphere. Their destruction would have unforeseeable consequences for water, weather, and temperature."

The discussion of the threat to the rain forests leads him
to a related issue: the growth in global population, often cited
as a major reason for cutting down rain forests.

"Certainly, the population question is among the
foremost," he says. It is unquestionably "going to be a central question of the 21st century," because the children who
will come to maturity early in that century have already
been born.

Does the Chinese policy of permitting only one child
per family offer a useful example?

"The Chinese are probably among the most successful
people to cope with the population-growth problem, and are
a most astonishing people." But, he adds, "I don't think their
policy will survive, in the sense that it is just too much against
human experience."

Yet von Weizsäcker says he sees little evidence that the
leading nations and institutions around the world are "really
contributing to an insight into these problems."

In this connection, he mentions in particular the Roman
Catholic Church as an organization that still could do more to
help solve these problems.

The discussion leads naturally to the issue of the social
and economic gap between the developing and the developed
countries—the so-called North-South divide.

"I think there has been too much talk about the possibilities of changing the world economic system, by which
the North-South problem could be solved. I don't believe
there *is* a world economic system which you can define, in a
sense, and say, 'Well, here it is.'"

He disagrees with those who say that the problem of
the massive debt burden in developing nations could be
solved by making the banks that have lent the money "feel a

responsibility for restoring or building a sound world economic system."

Private banks, he says, "exist for the purpose of lending money and earning money out of their interest." If Western governments have encouraged banks to lend money to the developing world, and if the debts turn out to be uncollectible, "then you have two possibilities: either to let the banks go bankrupt, or to pay back the money that cannot be paid back by the debtors through your government or our government."

It "will not work," for example, simply to assert that "the world's economic system is unjust and doesn't work"—and that banks must be taught "how to behave responsibly vis-à-vis the third-world."

Even this problem, in von Weizsäcker's eyes, is related to the natural world. What he terms "the very unjust distribution of chances between North and South"—and the related problem of developing-world debt—arise, in part, because "their raw materials don't get a good price."

But the fact is, he explains, that some of these raw materials are no longer in great demand. "So it doesn't help very much to deplore an unjust system in the pricing of a raw material no one needs." The need for the future, he suggests, is for an understanding of economics that goes far beyond tinkering with debt and pricing.

And how does energy figure into von Weizsäcker's thinking about the future?

"Energy supply is, of course, very important," he notes, although he adds that "it's easier to be solved" than the problems of population and environmental degradation.

But here, too, he argues that the issue is fundamentally a question of man's relation to nature, in that many energy-generating activities either degrade the environment or, as in the case of nuclear energy, pose what many consider to be unacceptable risks of accidental pollution.

At present, he says, the world "will not and cannot get out of nuclear energy." Instead, he says, "the main decision should be to concentrate all our efforts on other energy sources." As soon as other sources are found, he adds, "it is more likely that we will get out of nuclear energy."

He acknowledges that West Germany has a highly developed nuclear industry that can easily "stand worldwide competition." But he discounts the argument that in the next century so many countries will need nuclear energy that the industry should be encouraged to expand.

"The majority of those countries will probably not be able to afford nuclear-energy plants with the high standard of security that we require from our own plants today." Instead, he foresees less expensive alternative sources, such as solar energy, being developed for many countries.

The problem "requires from us *today*—not in fifteen years—a concentration, a very big effort, in financing and manpower and inducement for bright young people to work in the field of alternative energies.

"If we want results within thirty or fifty years, they will come only if we work with that kind of concentration *today*."

Thinking of nuclear energy leads von Weizsäcker to nuclear arms—and to world peace. How does that relate to his overriding concern for nature?

"Without peace in a nuclear age," he asserts, "it's not worth talking about preserving creation."

He cannot deny, he says, that the presence of nuclear weapons has had a healthy deterrent effect that "is preserving our peace" in Europe, as it has for the past forty years. "I think deterrence, basically, is an important and valid argument," he says, adding that some politicians only confuse the issue when they argue that deterrence is not "moral" and that peace can be preserved only by getting rid of "all those [nuclear] weapons."

Fundamentally, however, the issue of peace for von Weizsäcker reaches far beyond arms control. What he is searching for, in an intriguing and still undeveloped way, is an alternative to war itself.

"I believe it is not totally unthinkable that the kind of war that history has taught us up through the 20th century . . . is not the kind of power struggle that will characterize the next century.

"I don't think mankind, in its character, will change. And I don't think power struggles will be exterminated altogether. But it is possible that . . . the means to go ahead with this power struggle will not necessarily include war, a military war, as it did in history."

Finally, what does von Weizsäcker see on the moral and ethical horizon?

The word he uses to describe the current trend is *secularization*—which, he says, is "a strange and foreign word" for which the German language has no equivalent. He interprets the trend not so much as a threat to some already established "moral standard" that will "break down on our way into the 21st century" but rather as a promising sign of "our ability to find out that there is a real problem." It is, he says, "a positive and not a negative sign."

"People have a feeling that it is too difficult for them to understand life—not only individual life but also the common life. In a situation of secularization and of all those technical and political and social developments that we have been talking about," he adds, there needs to be a "strong effort to not only accompany [that process of development] but to guide it by some kind of moral or religious guideline.

"It is true that churches have more difficulties than they used to have." But those difficulties "are not a sign that more and more people would like to get rid of religion, but perhaps, on the contrary, that they are not satisfied with the churches' still fairly traditional ways of handling problems."

"It is in this sense," he says, that the society of the future will need to find "some general directions for how to live together"—for what he calls "the whole ethics of living, individually and socially."

Does he foresee, then, a society turning back to a lost ethical standard?

"I would not say 'turning back' but 'turning ahead,' " he concludes with a smile, "because it's not very easy to say 'turning back.' Where to? What kind of 'back'?"

An Agenda for the 21st Century

VII

One way or another, these twenty-two voices have spoken to nearly every issue of concern to humanity. Some talked about heady technological advances—the robots and electronics and genetics that will reshape daily life in the next century. Others focused on social, economic, and political trends—increased leisure, a heightening of international competitiveness, the burgeoning of the Asian nations, and a host of others. And some called for a higher vision of the heart, soul, and mind of humanity—better arts, finer journalism, sounder governance, greater compassion for the world's hungry and homeless.

But which are the first-intensity items—the "high leverage" issues (in former World Bank president Robert McNamara's phrase) to which humanity must devote its full attention and its unstinting resources? Six vital items seem to emerge:

- The threat of nuclear annihilation
- The danger of overpopulation
- The degradation of the global environment
- The gap between the developing and the industrial worlds
- The need for fundamental restructuring of educational systems
- The breakdown in public and private morality

The list is not in order of priority—although the nuclear issue appears to rank first. Nor did every item arise in every discussion. In some interviews, several items appeared under single headings—with population, environment, and the North-South gap often packaged into a bundle, for example, or morality and education lumped together. Most surprising, perhaps, is the absence of two key items from this list: energy resources and international debt. Several of the people interviewed, to be sure, argued strongly for these two points. To a number of others, however, these issues appeared problematic but not intractable.

Why these six? Here, in a nutshell, are some of the reasons.

Nuclear Annihilation

There is widespread agreement that, as long-time labor leader Douglas Fraser says, "the consequences of not doing something" about this subject could be "horrible . . . beyond imagination." Others note that, if this item is not satisfactorily addressed, none of the others will matter.

"This is an issue that, if we do not resolve it, will consume us," says Nigerian General Olusegun Obasanjo. Or, as West German president Richard von Weizsäcker puts it, "Without peace in a nuclear age, it's not worth talking about preserving creation."

Few see a nuclear holocaust as arising from a calculated, all-out conflict between the superpowers. Rather, the greater danger appears to be from an accident, an irrational reaction on the part of a world leader, or a lashing out by a small nation driven to desperation.

For several thinkers, however, the possibility of a future physical disaster is of less concern than the immediacy of the mental impact of living in a nuclear age. "Once you've said to people—and we have, to a whole generation—that you live in a world that can end at any moment," observes theater director Lloyd Richards, "it affects their sense of responsibility."

Or, as novelist Carlos Fuentes put it, "the consciousness that nature can disappear along with us . . . really shakes your soul."

Not surprisingly, the discussion of nuclear peril was interwoven with calls for rethinking of the basis of world peace—not as a standoff among frightened adversaries but as what philosopher Mortimer Adler calls "a positive condition," in which "individuals and peoples can solve all their problems, all their conflicts, by law and by talk rather than by force."

At bottom, says General Obasanjo, the need is "to understand ourselves through communication, and to be able to put ourselves across to ourselves in a way that we will be able to cooperate and reduce threat and fear."

Population
The scope of the population issue, unlike some of the others, can be assessed fairly accurately: All the people who will be approaching middle age in the early decades of the 21st century have already been born. Yet the real problem, except in some densely packed nations, is still in the future.

"You can live a civilized life with a much higher population density than we have in the United States," says physicist Freeman Dyson. He adds, however, that the world "can't go on growing at its present rate for very long." Yet size alone is not the problem. What causes the "human misery," as Robert McNamara explains, is "the imbalance of population growth rates on the one hand and social and economic advance on the other."

Much of the concern focuses on Africa—which, as historian Paul Johnson warns, is just now entering a surge of population growth. "There's going to be a great deal more growth and instability over the next thirty or forty years," he warns. "When you go through these terrific population surges, it always means a great deal of either imperialism or of political instability, revolution, and so on."

Left unchecked, says former president Jimmy Carter, that surge will produce "increased dissension, increased animosity, uncontrollable numbers of refugees, and an increased tendency toward revolution or violence." In fact, several thinkers see the population problem as the cause of most of the world's ills: third-world hunger, disease, poverty, energy insufficiency, environmental damage, a reshaping of international trade and banking, and immigration pressures.

Another sort of population shift—one that will have effects all across the industiral world—will come in the form of aging. By the end of the 21st century, says futurist Theodore Gordon, there will be substantial increases in "the number of people who will be much older than the oldest people today."

Environment

"Every possible agenda item you're going to mention," said President von Weizsäcker early in his interview, "has to do with my primary concern—namely, to preserve nature." For most of the people interviewed, the degradation of the environment comes second only to nuclear holocaust in its potential for destroying humanity and the natural world.

"This loss or deterioration of the natural world is probably the number one problem," says historian Barabara Tuchman. "I think it's already more with us than is the nuclear."

While some thinkers raise issues associated with the industrial world—such as acid rain, air and water pollution, and the destruction of the ozone layer—much of the concern centers on developing-world problems: the destruction of the rain forests, the erosion of topsoil through poor farming practices, the pollution of groundwater. Many draw clear connections between environmental and population problems. "The environment is going to determine, in the final analysis, what population can be supported," says business leader David Packard.

Standing at the juncture of the population-environment problem is the issue of food. The next century, says Theodore Gordon, will require "the complete revision of agriculture as we've known it." Noting that in the past "we've always grown food," he foresees an age of advanced genetics where self-replicating cells produce edible materials. "In other words, we will not necessarily be tied to land for production."

The North-South Gap
Here the problem is largely defined as a need to strike a difficult balance between opposing forces. For economist Marina Whitman the challenge is for developing nations to preserve national identity in a global marketplace. For University of Chicago president Hanna Gray, the problem is to "sustain both a world economy and the hopes for democratic and humanitarian governments . . . in the less-developed countries."

There is broad agreement that the developed nations need to be doing more to help their less-developed neighbors, not simply for altruistic reasons, but because, Jimmy Carter says, "We're all in the same boat." Unless such efforts are made, these thinkers generally feel that the problems of the South will spill over into the North. Unfortunately, the gap seems to be growing—"making the rich richer," as physicist Abdus Salam says, "and the poor hungry man's soul sink lower."

For General Obasanjo, the gap is not only between nations but often within nations—bringing the problem of poverty closer to home for the industrial nations. "Just as you have the North-and-South divide within the world," he says, so also "within each nation you have a certain amount of North and South."

How can the gap be closed? The group is divided. For some, the U.N. provides a promising model. Others, sharply critical of such supranational mechanisms, see more promise in a freeing of world markets, a strengthening of the economies in the developed world, and an invigoration of international trade. Many recognize that technology, rather than shrinking the gap, may stretch it—in part because most technologies, originated in the industrial nations, are meant to save rather than use labor. "There is a whole class of technology not yet discovered," says Theodore Gordon, "which may be big technology, but it is labor-intensive."

Education

Implicit in many of these discussions is the idea that if the world is to deal with the first four agenda items, it will need to undertake a strenuous reappraisal of the last two: education and morality.

Because the developed nations provide the educational leadership, much of the discussion focused on education in the industrial world. How, then, do these thinkers assess Western-style education?

"Our educational system is absolutely inadequate—not relatively but absolutely inadequate—for the purposes of democracy," asserts Mortimer Adler. Paul Johnson agrees. "One of the things we've got to do in the 21st century is to rethink the whole ideology of education," he says, noting, "Perhaps the most important thing that will happen in the 21st century is a rebirth of classical cultural values and civilization—after a century of frenzied experiment that hasn't really produced very much."

Most of the interviewees, when they talk of education, see significant changes coming: more developing-world students, older students, more lifelong education, more on-the-job training, more leisure time to pursue knowledge, more difficulty finding the bedrock of real wisdom under a blizzard of information. Hanna Gray says she finds it "astonishing" that so many undergraduates major in business—at the expense, she says, of learning about "basic science and the basic humanities and social sciences" in a liberal arts program. Michael Hooker, chancellor of the University of Maryland's

Baltimore County campus, agrees. "I'd educate everybody in the humanities—literature, philosophy, poetry," he says, because "they tell the truth."

Morality

Asked to characterize the present, Barbara Tuchman calls it "an Age of Disruption." And the greatest disruption, she says, is found in "the real deterioration of public morality." She touches on a theme that pervades these interviews. The failure of public truth telling, the sale of political influence, the acceptance of illegality in stock-market dealings—such topics appear again and again in these interviews, sometimes prominently and sometimes subtly. For social philosopher Sissela Bok, morality is the central issue for the 21st century: Because she sees "trust" as the vital missing ingredient in so many negotiations, she foresees a time when public officials will have to "take moral principles into account" in order to develop the trust necessary for negotiating toward solutions.

Closely related are questions of private morality. Marina Whitman sees, in the 21st century, a much greater need for the values of strong family life. Michael Hooker warns of a "growing intellectual and cultural and ethical anomie" in the teenage population. And Japanese educator Shuichi Kato observes, "Most people are not very much concerned, seriously, with other people's suffering. By and large it seems to me that the whole of society is geared to domination and manipulation—rather than to compassion."

To author and editor Norman Cousins the problem goes to the very core of survival: "We move into the 21st century without the philosophy or the sociology or the politics that can keep the species going." Yet sociologist Amitai Etzioni sees signs of change. "We've been for twenty years very me-istic, very, very strong on the individual, very neglectful of the we-ness. And we're having a comeback—not of collectivism, but of a better balance between the I and the we."

These, then, are the six items on the 21st century's agenda. Can humanity come to grips with them?

Few think the road ahead will be easy. "Things are going to get worse," says Mortimer Adler, "before they get better." Why? Because, according to many of these thinkers, humanity's current institutions are designed to cope only with current problems. The need, voiced repeatedly, is to redesign institutions—of government, education, economics, business, and so forth—to bring them into line with the pace and complexity of 21st-century challenges.

The current structures, many say, are simply not working. "When [problems] are not in a crisis stage," says David Packard, "no one pays any attention to them." Efforts to resolve long-term problems, says Jimmy Carter, come about "almost entirely as a reaction to crisis." Yet many would agree with Amitai Etzioni that the change involves attitudes rather than simply institutions. "In the end, you cannot police people," he says. "You have to make certain things unthinkable."

Beneath the surface of most of these discussions, however, lies a quiet optimism. "I really don't know enough to be a pessimist," says Norman Cousins, who describes himself as "optimistic about the intangibles that could be converted into assets."

Most of the people interviewed expressed a similar optimism. Lloyd Richards called it "perspective." Marina Whitman called it "balance." Hanna Gray saw it as "intellectual and personal integrity" in the face of "cheap and simple versions of life and history." Sissela Bok thought of it as "a virtuous circle" spiraling up out of "defeatism and passivity."

All of them expressed a sense of urgency—a concern that the problems were serious and that there was no time to waste. But most shared the conviction that there are plenty of ways forward—as long as humanity is sufficiently willing to undertake major changes. "We need a revolution of the mind," says Russian poet Andrei Voznesensky. "I'm not interested in the 21st century if it will be only robots. It can happen, but it will be death: We will be alive, but dead. And that is why I'm very eager about our art, about poetry. We need it like vitamins."

Perhaps, in the end, Carlos Fuentes spoke for the group when, in decrying the "great addiction to materialism," he touched on what he called "the moral rewards of progress."

"I am not against material progress," he said. "I am against the consciousness that material progress will solve our problems."

Fuentes could have put it another way. What most needs resisting, he might have said, is the consciousness that setting an agenda will solve our problems. By themselves, agendas never solve anything. Humanity is long on plans for accomplishing worthy goals—and even longer on complaints about the state of the world. In shorter supply are the conjunctions of social, political, and financial forces that transform plans into policy. But even those policies are of uncertain value without the qualities of thought—the "habits of the heart," to use a phrase that sociologist Robert Bellah borrowed from Alexis de Tocqueville—that bring about solutions.

What are those characteristics? Interestingly enough, the six agenda items defined here provide some of their own answers. Woven through the language of these interviewees is a concern not just for the agenda items themselves but for the human qualities that will steer us toward progress.

One such quality is trust. One cannot, for instance, take up serious work on negotiations concerning the nuclear threat without a considerable amount of trust—both in terms of one's own trustworthiness and a trustfulness of one's partners. How a nation develops a fuller sense of trust, then, is a vital question along the road to lessening the nuclear threat.

Nor, as several interviewees point out, can one begin to resolve the issues of the North-South divide or the challenge of excessive population growth without first deepening one's compassion for those who face poverty, hunger, disease, and hopelessness. One can hardly engage in meaningful education reform, or stem the degradation of the environment, without a growing recognition of the dignity and worth of man—and an increasing respect for the natural context in which humanity lives. Finally, one cannot begin to address the breakdown in public and private morality without an increasing sense of obedience—to the enforceable laws of society, certainly, but more importantly to those values and standards that are unenforceable.

Trust, compassion, dignity, obedience: In these terms, and in similar ones scattered throughout this book, one finds the beginnings of an entirely different sort of agenda. It runs parallel to the formal agenda. But it addresses itself to the personal and the private. Where the six items on the formal agenda look outward, the characteristics on the personal agenda look inward. And where the formal agenda involves world-scale problems sometimes daunting in their complexity, the personal agenda addresses issues that face each individual in every walk of life.

At bottom, then, this book asks a single question: How can we have a better 21st century? Part of the answer lies in the work that must be done by the relatively small number of people in leadership positions, acting both locally and globally on the major items on the formal agenda. But the other part of the answer lies in the willingness of each individual to act on the personal agenda.

If we are to make the next century an age worth inhabiting, we will not do so simply by resolving, from the top down, the issues on the formal agenda. We will do it because individuals everywhere, taking to heart the personal agenda, are building within themselves a sounder society from the ground up. That act of building, happening within private lives across the world, ultimately charts a way to resolve the issues on the agenda for the 21st century.

Illustration Credits

Olusegun Obasanjo. Courtesy of William Goidell.

David Packard. Courtesy of William Goidell.

Lloyd Richards. Courtesy of *The Christian Science Monitor*, Peter Main.

Abdus Salam. Courtesy of Foto Scrobogna.

Barbara W. Tuchman. Courtesy of Peter Tobia.

Richard von Weizsäcker. Courtesy of Sven Simon.

Andrei Voznesensky. Courtesy of *The Christian Science Monitor*, Robert Harbison.

Marina Whitman. Courtesy of Russ Marshall.

Index

Entries in UPPER CASE indicate the six major agenda items identified in the final chapter.

Dyson on, 117, 120–122
Gray on, 63–66
Johnson on, 60
Kato on, 24–25
Obasanjo on, 172–173
Einstein, Albert, 109
Eisenhower, Dwight D., 40, 111
El Salvador, 178
Eminent Persons Group (Commonwealth Mission to South Africa), 168
Employment, changes in, 89–93
Energy
  dearth of, 8, 21–22, 29, 72, 134–135, 185, 188–189, 195–196
  future sources of, 116
  nuclear, 134–135, 189
  solar, 22, 189
  ENVIRONMENTAL DEGRADATION, 195, 198–199
  Adler on, 8
  Carter on, 178–179
  Cousins on, 39
  Johnson on, 59
  Kato on, 22
  McNamara on, 102–103
  Obasanjo on, 171–172
  Packard on, 132–133
  Tuchman on, 46, 48
  von Weizsäcker on, 185–191
  Voznesensky on, 151
Ethiopia, 180
Etzioni, Amitai
  biography, 69–70
  Capital Corruption, 69
  Immodest Agenda, An, 69
  interview with, 69–76
  mentioned, 37, 79
  quoted, 201–202
Europe
  Eastern, 59. See also Czechoslovakia

Western, 56–57, 136. See also France, Germany, Federal Republic of, Great Britain, Netherlands, Spain

Family, 85–86, 122
Fantasia, 131
Fisher, H. A. L., 167
Food. See also Hunger
  distribution of, 180
  production of, 23, 29, 129
Ford Motor Company, 96, 97
France, 121
Fraser, Douglas
  biography, 88–89
  interview with, 88–95
  mentioned, 79
  quoted, 196
Fraser, Malcolm, 168
Friedman, Milton, 84
Fuentes, Carlos
  biography, 157–158
  Death of Artemio Cruz, The, 157
  interview with, 157–164
  mentioned, 141
  Old Gringo, The, 157
  quoted, 196, 203
  Terra Nostra, 157
  Where the Air Is Clear, 157

Gallup, George Jr., xx–xxi
Gandhi, Mohandas, 13–14
Geldof, Bob, 114
General Motors, 79, 85, 87
Genetic technology, 125–126, 195. See also Biotechnology
Germany, Federal Republic of, 90, 91, 114, 178, 184
Glasnost, 155
Global 2000, Inc., 176
Goethe, Johann Wolfgang von, 57

Voznesensky, Andrei (*cont.*)
  Juno and Perchance, 150
  mentioned, 141
  quoted, 203
  Stained-Glass Craftsman, 149

Wagner, Richard, 25
Watergate, 54
White House Science Council,
  132, 135
Whitman, Marina
  biography, 79–80
  interview with, 79–87
  mentioned, 79
  quoted, 199, 201, 202
Williams, Raymond, xxi
Women, role of, 51–52
Women's movement, 67–68
Woodcock, Leonard, 88
World Bank, 96, 97, 100
World Court, 17
World government, 9, 41, 98

Yevtushenko, Yevgeny, 149
Young, David R., xx
Youngstown, (Ohio), 93